There's Something Going On!

Walking the Camino de Santiago

SIMON DONLEVY

THE CHOIR PRESS

First published in the United Kingdom in 2020 by
The Choir Press

ISBN 978-1-78963-158-06

To Lisa.

Thank you for your whole hearted support for my crazy ideas.

I love you.

v

Contents

There's Something Going On!

The path didn't start as you'd think in St Jean,
'cause the spiritual journey had already begun.
For Neil, it was special and had to be done;
he knew it would be tough, yet he hoped for some fun.
Walking alone, carrying his load,
nearly 800 k on this rugged open road,
thirty-three days apart from his wife,
one for each year of Jesus' life,
though a small price to pay for him to discover
a pilgrim's life, and the first week with his brother.
There's something going on!

Walking west, sun on his back,
meagre belongings in his backpack,
soon to discover it's not just a walk;
despite the long distance the key is to talk.
Complete strangers will tell of their deepest hell,
but are there to feel safe, and trust in their faith,
to the point that a hug or warm embrace
gives a look deep inside and behind every face.
There's a story to be told deep from within,
to inspire us all or be thankful therein.
There's something going on!

Brother Martin departed after day seven,
but Catherine and Jacqueline, 'angels from Heaven',
were sent to provide further moral support,
to see him through; to avoid an abort.
And the family got bigger, and bigger it grew,
with Carlos and Søs to name just a few.
Whether you're on your own or part of a team,
help is on hand to achieve your dream.
One is never alone on the Camino;
someone's always with you on the road to Santiago.
There's something going on!

So two friends went to see what the fuss was about,
Simon and Bruce; for two days they did sprout,
a 'family' welcome – like they'd all met before.
They went for a walk but came back with much more.
For they did not expect such a short time on the track
to hit them for six and have such an impact,
such wonderful people all heading one way
with a party in León: by the cathedral, you say?
There's something going on!

This historic route is not hard to follow;
you look for the shell, or arrow in yellow,
but that's the easy part of this incredible feat;
it's not so simple with blisters on your feet.
Cold winds in the morns and the bitterest gales,
so Neil keeps warm with the 'dragon hat' from Wales.
Whilst Carlos had sent his pack to the albergue,
the cold was severe and he feared hypothermia.
That wise man from Porto was struggling that morn,
freezing, without layers, so Neil's fleece adorned.
There's something going on!

After tough days in the mountains, Neil arrives wearily
at Cruz de Ferro with gifts from his family.
He adds to the stones that have lain there for years,
an emotional moment as he fights back the tears,
thinking of home and the ones that he loves,
gaining strength from their love and the force from above.
There's something going on!

He's nearly there now; compostela's in view
for Mr O'Toole and his newly formed crew.
He's battled the mountains, the cold and the snow,
and today he has just 100 k to go.
He'll soon be in the arms of his true love Elaine,
a few days in Santiago, and then home on a plane.
There's something going on!

The last weeks will feel like they've gone in a whirl
once he gets back to Cardiff and cuddles his girls.
One day this will make a great story for Mari,
who as yet doesn't know how amazing is Grampy!
But he'll share the lessons away from the road,
in everyday life to unburden the load,
and we should all learn from Neil, and this holy ground,
to want nothing . . .
apart from those you can throw your arms around.

There's something going on!

Simon Donlevy

Introduction

If you'd known me before I wrote that poem, you'd think I'd gone completely mad. I'd never written a poem before. I'm not a deeply religious man either. In fact, other than attending for the occasional celebratory passage, marriage or carriage, I tend to avoid entering churches at any cost; they give me the creeps.

The cause of all this is, I believe, deeply rooted in my childhood. I was scarred for life at the age of five by the haunting image of Robert Powell being nailed to a cross, playing Jesus of Nazareth. I had nightmares about it for years. It was the eyes. I'm now forty-nine, and that image still haunts me.

However, something has happened in the last eighteen months that's starting to make me want to face my demon. Not that I really think I should be referring to Jesus as a demon, particularly in a story that's predominantly about a pilgrimage.

So, is there really something going on?

What I'm about to embark upon is born of an inquisitive mind, a restlessness about something intangible, maybe even a calling. Some might just see it as a good old-fashioned midlife crisis. Either way, it's going to be an adventure. Whilst I know where I'm heading, and how I'm supposed to get there, I'm not totally convinced I'm going to make it. It involves walking nigh on 500 miles (800 kilometres), alone, and carrying my own gear. Plus I only have little legs!

It's not about the destination, but the journey itself.

Fancy coming with me?

PART ONE

Before

CHAPTER ONE

I'll Walk the Camino in Retirement

I have experienced the Camino for three days, which is what inspired me to write the poem. I'll tell you more about why I was there later, but at that moment I fell in love with it. I made a commitment to myself that I would walk the Camino when I retire.

And then it hit me, one morning in April 2018, as I was on my morning commute to work in London.

Why wait?

I might not be well enough when I retire. Let's face it, I might not even live that long; one never knows what life has in store for us. So I started to wrestle with it:

'Could I possibly take five weeks out?'

But you only get five weeks' holiday all year.

'Why don't I take a sabbatical for a few months?'

But you can't afford it.

Over the following days I kept internalising it, asking myself if I could justify not earning, and I kept coming back to this simple point: I'd worked for Lloyds Bank for thirty years. In that time the biggest breaks I'd ever had were two three-week-long holidays, and the last one had been ten years ago. The longest period I'd ever had off work was four weeks thanks to viral meningitis back in 2001 – which, believe me, was no holiday.

Surely I deserved some 'me time'. Could we make it work?

I came home that evening and discussed it with Lisa. It's always easy to do things like that. We never keep anything from each other, particularly our feelings and emotions, so when something like this needs to be discussed I don't have to give it any prep time or wait for the ideal moment to drop it into the conversation. I walked through the front door, gave her a kiss and said, 'I've had a bit of an idea.'

Since then she's been nothing but supportive. What started out as taking a few weeks off work on sabbatical has turned into a proper break. My boss agreed to a full six months starting in May next year. That at least gives us a year to try to save so we can survive without my salary for the period. Thankfully Lisa also works, so that really helps. I keep joking with her, telling her she has to keep me in the manner to which I've become accustomed!

It's on; this thing is really happening.

September: The beach

I'm with Lisa, sipping an ice-cold beer at the end of a hot day in a beautiful bay. We're on holiday in Sardinia. We've been swimming in Porto Torres and chilling on the beach; it's 6 pm and we're now in a bar overlooking the beach, watching the sun fall over the horizon. It's only the second time we've been able to get away for a fortnight outside the school holidays without the kids. I say 'kids'; Michael is now twenty-three, working, having graduated with a first-class degree in Mathematics from Bath University, and James (Jimbo), who's eighteen, is about to start university at Surrey the week after we get back. He's also a mathematician. I'm not sure where they get a head for figures from; Lisa is a bookkeeper and I've been in banking for thirty years!

I'm sitting here reading John Brierley's guidebook on the Camino de Santiago for the second time. I've just decided to capture my story, so I've begun by writing this text on my phone, with a view to embellishing it later. This will be a story, my story, for my family, friends and, of course, me. A legacy, if you like, about a small chapter in my life, but hopefully a big part of it. My hope is it should write itself over the next few months and, with some luck, would also be interesting to others. I guess that will all depend on what transpires.

I've already decided I will start my pilgrimage in May next year, going alone. People have started to ask me 'Why?' and to be completely honest with you, as of now, three months after I decided to take this path (see what

3

I did there?), I still don't really know. That might seem strange. It feels really odd to me too.

I think Lisa and the boys think I've gone a bit crazy and/or I'm going to become a hippy. It might be both, but the chances of me growing long hair are well gone. Before we came on holiday, I overheard Jimbo talking to Michael. 'I think Mum and Dad are going through a midlife crisis; Mum's joined the pub choir and Dad's going on a walk to find God.' They both knew I was within earshot too!

I have just explained to Lisa that I've written a few paragraphs of my story and I offered to read it to her. To my surprise she told me not to. Instead she came up with a great idea and suggested that she might write one as well, giving her version of events and capturing her thoughts. I'm not sure how that will work, but it might work out a treat. We agreed it would be fun to compare the two versions one day after this chapter in our lives has ended.

CHAPTER TWO

People

The people in my story are real people, and any comments are made with sincerity, affection and love. They are also a thank-you for being an important part of my journey and consequently appearing here. I'll apologise now should I happen to upset anyone. I really hope I won't.

I'll introduce many people to you on my journey, some of whom I obviously haven't even met yet. Some will be inspiring and some will be wacky, I'm sure. I should start with some very important people in my life now, and there's no one more important to me than Lisa.

Lisa

Love is the fuel of life. My life is Lisa. You'll have gathered that Lisa's my wife, but she's also my best friend. I won't bore you, but she is the fuel that gives me the energy and desire to get out of bed each day. I love her with all of me. None of what I have achieved in life would have been possible without her, and everything that I will do, or become, will be because of her. She just so happens to be one of life's most beautiful and caring human beings. OK, so I've gone on a bit.

Mum

She lives in the West Midlands, some 180 miles away, so we don't get to see her as much as we'd like. She's really excited for me but doesn't really have any notion of what is involved. Every time I call her, she asks me if I'm still doing the Campino! She's not good at remembering names in her immediate family, let alone places in Spain!

She keeps asking me if Lisa is going to be OK whilst I'm away, and I never really know how to answer it. I think it must be a generation thing. She's a wonderful mum and I know she's genuinely asking out of love and affection, but there's a part of me that just wants to say, 'Actually, Mum, that's a really good point. I haven't thought about Lisa at all. I'll call the whole thing off!'

I love my mum dearly. She's not had an easy life and has done so much for me that I couldn't begin to express it here – there's a whole book there in itself. She never, ever puts herself first. She's completely selfless, summed up more than anything by how she retired early to nurse her own mum at home, despite not really having the income to do so. Sometimes I wish she would be more selfish, but caring is an integral part of her DNA. She likes to fuss and worry about people. She's now worrying about me being on my own for so long, getting lost or injured or even both.

So, when she came to stay with us recently, Lisa and I had the great idea to sit with her one evening and watch *The Way*, a beautiful film about a man who walks the Camino. We thought it would give her an insight into what I was about to undertake and provide her with some reassurance. Unfortunately the premise for the film is that the main character's son dies attempting to cross the Pyrenees during bad weather, but we forgot about that bit! So, rather than finding some comfort, she now thinks I'm going to die, either through boredom or, apparently, from an injury that renders my legs useless and leaves me rotting away in a ditch, below soaring vultures, whilst frantically trying to get a mobile phone signal. I keep reassuring her that I am only going to Spain and there will be lots of other people around; that it'll be May and June, when the weather is better. But she's a mum, my mum, and I guess it's a mother's duty to worry about her offspring. Talking of which . . .

Richard

My crazy younger big-little brother. We're not close in the sense that we speak to each other every day, but we are very close in other ways. He is my brother, after all. Fortunately he lives near Mum, which gives us some reassurance.

Rich and his wife Jo are really busy with work, and when not working they're taxiing their daughter Millie around from one dance training session or competition to another. I'd love to see more of them. I make an effort to see them every time I go to Mum's. Sometimes I play golf with him, or if we're lucky my visit will coincide with when our football team, Wolverhampton Wanderers, are playing at home and we'll go and watch the game.

Without fail we have a blast whenever we're together. Rich has a real zest for life; he's funny, always cracking jokes and simply loves being the centre of attention, and some! It's always entertaining when he's around, and my boys adore their crazy Uncle Rich. We're always inviting them down to stay. I want to take him around my local golf course and buy him a pint or two in my local pub. He's just had a career change, so I'm hoping he'll have a bit more time and we'll see more of them.

Father figures

I don't really have anyone I can call a father, but safe to say Rich and I have had a few over the years! I'm not seeking sympathy, but, cutting a long story short, my real father walked out on us when I was five. We were living in Nigeria at the time and it must have been so traumatic for Mum. I'm glad to say that Mum remarried a few years later. Her new husband was Ralph, who was like my best mate for twelve years, until he decided his future lay elsewhere and left us just before my eighteenth birthday.

Throughout this whole period there was, however, one man who was my constant idol: my Uncle Ken. He was always there for me. He always took time to listen, he gave me advice when I needed it and his counsel was always spot-on. He helped me with my interviews and it's down to him that I joined the management trainee scheme with Lloyds Bank in 1988. I loved that man and looked up to him so much, but he sadly passed away about twenty years ago, leaving a void no one could fill.

At the age of nineteen I left home to live with Lisa in Brighton. Thankfully Mum had since met Alan, so I wasn't leaving her on her own. For thirty years he made Mum happy, as they shared their lives together. Sadly he too passed away on Easter Sunday in 2017.

Lisa's dad, Roger, has been a real father figure to me too, not that he deliberately tried to fill anyone's shoes. It just happened. I guess this has partly been because I've lived near him and partly because he's just a decent bloke.

7

He's also a perfectionist, particularly when it comes to DIY. This is not a great position to be in when you're starting out in life with your first new home. I was always nervous doing any jobs around the house. If I was putting a shelf up, or hanging curtains, I knew it would have to be dead level as it would come under his scrutiny at some point. He always took an interest, but as time went on I realised he was not being critical; he was simply trying to get the balance right between interfering and encouraging. I soon learned that getting him involved is the best option; not only is he a grafter but he almost always has the right tool for the job. Somewhere in his magic workshop (a small TARDIS-like shed that seems to stock the amount of stuff they have in B&Q), he'll have a new machine, spare part or gadget that is always ideal for the job at hand. He's always prepared to help me (and my brother-in-law Chris, too), which normally gives him the chance to show off his latest rechargeable power tools.

I've always ignored the hurt that having two father figures walk out on me created; after all, I have my own family now, and that's the best medicine. Maybe, just maybe, I'll spend some time contemplating this a little more whilst I'm putting one foot in front of the other along the path to Santiago.

Peggy

Peggy is my mother-in-law and, of course, Roger's wife. Many people hate their mother-in-laws. Quite simply, I wouldn't change mine for the world.

The Crokes

Cara is Lisa's sister, married to Chris Croke. They have two beautiful girls, Lucy (eleven) and Ella (six), whom I dote on. They live ten doors away from us and we're all incredibly close. It's quite special. We all hold a 'family first' virtue close to our hearts and it will never be any different. What is lovely is that my boys are very close to the girls too, despite a big age difference.

Neil

Outside my family life is yet another father figure. Neil. He was a senior director in Lloyds before he retired with Parkinson's a few years ago. I got to know Neil through an outdoor adventure competition at the bank. I didn't work for him then; in fact I didn't know how senior he was until much later, when he called me to ask me for some information for an interview he had for a director's role. That typifies the make of the man; he is humble and gracious but the smartest and most astute man I've ever worked with, a true leader by any standards. I eventually joined his team and he's given me a lot of guidance and counsel along the way for which I will be forever grateful.

Overall, I've worked with him on and off, in different roles, for about twelve years. He drove a hard bargain and had high standards of delivery, but he was always fair and I always knew what I was working on and, more importantly, why. Many of today's leaders, in any industry, could learn so much from him.

So, having retired with the devastating news that he had Parkinson's, one thing Neil wanted to do was walk the Camino. I'd never heard of it. I thought he was going on a little hike in the sun somewhere. Over the weeks that followed, in the lead-up to his Camino, I learned so much more, and also how much importance this would have for him, as a Catholic.

I have a small group of friends and we all know Neil very well. We've also had the benefit of his leadership and coaching in various guises. We call ourselves the Midge Ure club (long story, but we were all a little bit drunk one Christmas and we were planning a summer break together in mid-June; someone heard 'Midge Ure' – it stuck!). Anyway, once we got a better understanding of the scale of the task that Neil was about to undertake, we were, to say the least, a little concerned.

So Bruce and I decided we'd go out in the middle of Neil's Camino, to check on him, support him and hopefully keep him motivated knowing we'd be with him at some point. We hoped it might also provide some reassurance to his wife, Elaine, knowing we'd be seeing him. We could also take some gear out for him or bring back any stuff he didn't need.

When we arrived, it was apparent that he was absolutely fine and we needn't have worried. He was being well and truly looked after by two angels whom he'd bumped into on the Camino; it was almost as though they'd been sent to look after him.

I too got so much out of those three days that when I returned ... well, you know the rest; you've read my poem and it was the spark that inspired this adventure. It really felt like there was something going on out there.

Stuart

Actually, I lied; I'm not walking all of it alone. Stu's a friend. We met through football. His son Cam played in the team that I used to coach.

Most of life's great ideas start in a pub. This was no different. We were chatting over a couple of beers and before we knew it he was coming out to walk with me for the last two weeks. Awesome.

I love Stu's outlook on life. He's incredibly observational and eloquent. What he witnesses in life is often followed with a witty line from a film or other historic quote, adding some well-timed humour to any occasion. I remember him saying once, 'If God is so all-encompassing then why did he make me an atheist?' He also thinks Christmas would be so much better if we could just remove some of the emphasis on religion. He's ready-made for the Camino, and I just know more will come out along the way.

Albergue

Whilst not a character as such, albergues warrant their own introduction because they play an integral part in any Camino. They are a sweet concept: cheap and cheerful accommodation, available only to pilgrims, all headed one way – Santiago. Sounds lovely, eh? But I've already experienced a few and they vary significantly in quality. There are also constant stories and fears of bed bugs.

Neil tells me that for the few days I was with him, we stayed in probably the worst albergues of his whole trip, but I think he's just trying to make me feel better. At one point on that trip I lay awake at 2.30 am. I was in a room filled with eighty men in bunk beds. We were in a convent in León; it was a snoring and farting cacophony! It was a laugh or cry situation, so I decided to see the funny side of it, but then couldn't stop laughing. The irony of it was that one bloke snoring his head off in the bunk opposite me was disturbed by my giggling. He woke, looked at me with a hint of disdain and then went back to sleep. I chuckled some more.

CHAPTER THREE

Preparation and Training

I've started training. I've learned a valuable lesson already. Blisters seem to like me.

Stu and I did a short walk with Lisa on the South Downs, six miles to a pub in Findon, and I got two little blisters. Six miles! They were painful, too. How will I manage 500 miles?

I've talked to many people about it, all with conflicting advice: boots tight; boots loose; tighten them downhill and loosen them uphill; wear a second thin pair of socks underneath your socks; apply Vaseline, never apply Vaseline; change your socks frequently; never wear two pairs of socks. It goes on. I think I'm just going to have to try them all out till I can walk a good distance without the little blighters appearing.

Christmas

Work Christmas parties always involve Secret Santa presents. This year the team is gathered in Bristol and it's fair to say we're all looking forward to it. It's been a particularly tough year. We're ready to let our hair down, that's for sure.

This was the first year I wasn't given a rude, albeit usually hilarious, gift. For example, one year I received a tomato grow bag with two foot-shaped patterns marked out on it, along with instructions:

1) cut along dotted line,
2) plant feet in holes,

3) water, and
4) wait to grow.

I'm not particularly tall, and as such my height has often been a good source of banter. To be honest, I thought this was genius; some real thought had gone into it.

Anyway, this year's present was one better. It was also surprisingly sincere. Secret Santa (AKA Gemma) had created an embossed journal for me to record my memoirs in. I was genuinely shocked, and equally quite touched. No piss-taking for a change either; there's definitely something going on!

*

In your late forties, receiving socks for Christmas is an expected norm: a traditional present for any middle-aged bloke. Let's be honest, socks make for a *really* boring Christmas present! We're all kids at heart; there's nothing better than opening an exciting present, and, frankly, socks don't fall into that category. Well, it transpires that this year they do.

I've been given proper hiking socks. I'm delighted and secretly excited about trying them out to see if they prevent my pain bubbles from reappearing. I've also been given gift cards and money for any additional gear that I need, so I'm going to get online in the January sales and buy the walking poles and backpack I've had my eye on.

28 December: Kit dilemma

How complicated can choosing the right backpack be? The biggest problem was deciding on size. Do I go for sixty litres or less?

Just before Christmas I had a meal with Neil and Søs, whom I met with Neil on the Camino last year. Neil told me that if I took a big backpack, I'd just fill it. To him weight was everything. Both he and Søs couldn't stress this enough, so I followed their advice and ordered a thirty-eight-litre one! It arrives on 4 January. I'm worried about whether it will be big enough to stow all the kit I need.

Neil said I shouldn't take any T-shirts, but two long-sleeved merino base layers that I can roll the sleeves up on when it is hot. I should take two pairs of pants and trousers/shorts, preferably the zip-off variety, a fleece, a waterproof, a sun hat and socks. That's it!

Apparently, the best approach is to wear one set of clothes, get to your albergue, put on your one and only clean set whilst you wash the dirty set, then wear the same clothes when you get up in the morning. Walk, arrive, repeat. A pilgrim's lifestyle is supposed to be a meagre one, I guess.

I went for another training walk with Stu and he told me that he's booked into a decent hotel in León when he flies out to meet me. I'll be entering the fourth week of my walk by then, and the thought of a hotel room, hot showers, clean towels and sheets already sounds appealing, but I'm on a budget and doing this the real way. Well, that's the theory, as I sit here in my slippers in my centrally heated study writing this.

New Year's Eve

I've got an exciting year ahead of me, but Lisa's nursing a cold and I'm on antibiotics for a chest infection. We both feel really lousy. We'd bought tickets to see our favourite local band and we also had VIP access, but we simply aren't well enough to go. Still, I turned this to my advantage and used the time to do some research for some more gear.

I've also been toying with raising money for charity. It seems a great thing to do at the turn of the year, with resolutions and all that, but then again if I raise money it will surely just add pressure on me to complete the walk. I can't quite decide right now.

My Spanish lessons start again on Monday, and I really need to knuckle down with these and practise more between lessons. I started them in September, as I decided the least I could do was try to learn some of the local language to get by, more out of courtesy than anything else. That's one of my new year's resolutions. There are a few others, intended to help me shed some of the excess making up the thirteen-stone four-pound figure that I was horrified to see when I stepped on the scales this morning. If I can't shed it this year, I never will, but I'm determined to hit my twelve-and-a-half-stone pre-walk target weight in May. They say you should write your goals down, so there you have it: one of mine in print.

Amazingly Stu has secured a new job and it is next door to where I work in Hove. This has given us a fantastic opportunity to develop a training plan.

He suggested we walk back from work sometimes during the darker winter months. It's 12.7 miles, which is a long way after a day at work. I suggested we start off by getting the train to a station five miles from home, walk home, then each week extend it a little further by getting the train but getting off a stop earlier. Our enthusiasm soon got the better of us, though. We walked eleven miles home last night, took a slight detour and enjoyed it, but my left foot is hurting today (plantar fasciitis) and I really don't feel like doing any more walking again today; that's not going to be an option on the Camino. That said, it felt good to have done it.

So next week we've decided to walk the whole way from Hove.

4 January: It's here

My backpack's here. I love it, and it feels really light and comfortable. I keep looking at it and thinking I've bought one too small. Surely that can't be big enough for five weeks on the road. I guess the mantra 'if you get a bigger one you'll fill it' will come into its own at the end of some very long days; I certainly hope so.

23 January: Hove to home

We set off in temperatures hovering around zero degrees and with the forecast of rain, sleet or snow. The forecast did not disappoint; we had all three and we got very cold and wet. This was, however, a great opportunity to try out my new wet weather gear. I also took my new backpack with some weight in it; only a couple of kilos, nothing like what I'll need for the walk, but it was a start. It was a chance to discover how waterproof everything actually was! It was also an opportunity to test our spirits through prolonged walking, head down into an icy wind, trying to keep the rain and snow out of our eyes. I know that can be soul-destroying.

None of it; we loved it. We felt alive. We were making the most of a miserable winter's evening.

At first, we kidded ourselves that to the rush hour traffic we must have looked like a couple of SAS soldiers out training in bleak conditions. The reality was, as we drew nearer home at about 10 pm, we just looked like two tired dodgy geezers who were on their way home after a drink, and the passing public would more likely be asking, 'Why have they taken their backpacks to the pub?'

I awoke this morning with severe foot pain again. I might need to get some treatment for it. There's no way I would want to walk any real distance on it today, but at least training is well underway.

By the way, if you think it took us too long to walk twelve and a half miles last night, I have to confess it is because we had to stop in Shoreham for some well-earned pasta and a glass of vino tinto at the local Italian restaurant. It was, after all, very cold and would have been rude not to. A man's gotta eat, but I accept that this isn't exactly the approach we'll need for the life of a true pilgrim, so that aspect of my training needs some work.

The good news is I now know where my waterproofs leak, which is nowhere. They were brilliant and kept me totally dry. However, the same couldn't be said for my backpack. Conclusion: I need to buy a backpack cover; more expense.

4 February

I've had some fantastic news today. I initially got invited to a mini-Camino WhatsApp group and wondered what was going on. It transpires my friends Neil, Jay and Bruce have arranged to come out to be with me for three days, when I'll be eight days into my walk. I'm absolutely thrilled and delighted. That is true friendship. It will give me something to aim at for the first week, and then, when they are gone, I will only have another one and a half weeks until Stu joins me. It's already starting to feel more doable; well, mentally, anyway. I'm still having trouble with my foot, however.

13 February

We had a four-way video call tonight, just to sort out logistics, kit etc., primarily for Bruce and Jay. They are both seasoned walkers; in fact, Jay has been on many pilgrimages and even trekked in the Himalayas. We also needed to sort out their flights and train times, and they needed to know where I anticipated my location would be eight days into my walk.

We agreed on a plan to meet near the town of Logroño. Neil, who has walked this route twice, was able to lend some of his knowledge of the area. Being a director at his level required a certain determination, drive and a little stubbornness, coupled with an uncanny ability to influence and get people to follow you. Despite the fact that he's been retired for three years now he still has this knack, and he does it without realising. He explained to me how fantastic it would be if I were to meet them in the small town of Viana just before Logroño, and I found myself buying in to it; how does he do that?

To be fair, he also stressed that it is my Camino and ultimately, wherever I am on day eight, they will find me. There's a small part of me, though, that doesn't want to disappoint him, so I'll still aim to be in Viana. Having looked at the map, it also means that they will then spend the next day with me crossing over into Rioja country, and that can only mean one thing, surely!

I do, however, want to take a moment to reflect and capture on record what this means to me. These are very dear friends and I'm privileged to have them in my life. We've all known each other for many years and we've done some great things together. But this is real commitment. Bruce has a young family; Jay has other commitments this year as he's going to India and also coming out with me to watch the Tour de France in July. For them to find the time, money and holiday from work and dedicate this to me for a few days is incredible and I will be forever grateful to them, as I am to their wives, Joely and Sangeeta.

As for Neil, well, he just loves the Camino. He's caught the bug and I know a part of him wants to be there to help and guide and impart his knowledge, and I'll happily accept it all. Thanks to Elaine (his wife) for her support, as this means Neil will be extending his current trip to be with me.

The kit is coming together now, but I've still got some critical decisions to make. Do I take boots and walking trainers or do I take walking trainers with walking sandals? Oh, the vicissitudes of life. Still, it is giving me a nice distraction from work at the moment, particularly as we're just agreeing our objectives for the year. I had a wry smile as I wrote mine, knowing I'm only going to be around until the end of April.

As for work, it is a strange feeling at the minute. I usually start each year at full speed and throw myself headlong into my work, trying to get a head start on my deliverables. I'm doing the same now, but it is like a condensed year insomuch as I'm focused on delivery and organising the team so that they are in as good a shape as possible for when I leave. The good news is that my boss has advertised for a secondment to replace me for six months. I have already had three people contact me to find out more about my role, and I would happily leave any of them at the helm.

The only slight concern I have at the minute is that there's rumour of another restructure coming. This means I might have to reapply for my job, or end up being placed into another role or being made redundant.

I have stopped worrying about it, though. Maybe it's because Mike has left home and is independent, which means I've only got to get James through another two years of university now, so it's not like I have a young family to support anymore. Maybe even planning on walking the Camino and taking six months off has already changed my mindset, a bit more accepting of fate and that everything happens for a reason; that's what Mum has always said to me. Maybe the chance to do something different may one day just get forced upon me; maybe I won't even want to go back.

Despite all of this, I really don't want redundancy, this year more than ever. I want these six months so that I can completely switch off from work and at least know I have something to go back to in November when I can start to earn some money again. Yes, redundancy would give me money now, but the problem is I would then just be without work, between jobs, and would have to spend the time I have earmarked as 'me time' worrying about finding a new job. And it is always easier to find employment when you're already in a job than when you're not. So I'll have faith that this won't happen to me this year.

Maybe after my sabbatical I'll be begging for redundancy, though I doubt it; I've always enjoyed working at Lloyds. I hope I'll be refreshed and ready to come back. It will definitely make me more appreciative of my monthly salary, having not received it for six months.

What is comforting, and always has been, is that whatever happens I know Lisa is behind me. We have a lovely family home and we're so happy in it, but she's always said, 'It is only a house, and home can be wherever we want it to be.' Should we ever need to sell it and buy something smaller, she wouldn't hesitate to do it. Little touches like this take the pressure off life and it's why I love her so much.

19 February

Do I raise money for charity? I've been giving this a lot of thought over the last few weeks. What if I do this and then injure myself and I can't finish? Fundraising just piles on the pressure to complete the walk, and the whole idea is to move away from pressure and stress. The easier question to answer was 'if I did raise money, whom would I raise it for?' and that didn't require much thought at all.

My niece Lucy is visually impaired. She's twelve now and is a real inspiration. She just throws herself into stuff, and when we all realised that she had a significant visual impairment we were all shocked but equally amazed by how she had been able to do the things she had done. The simple fact is, through courage and bravado and not really knowing any different, she just got on with life. It took a while for Cara and Chris to get to grips with it; it's hard for any parent to accept that their child may be just a little different from others.

Look Sussex is a local charity and they have been brilliant for Lucy and her family. They've helped them to realise just how fortunate they actually are and have also provided them with a great support network, emotionally as well as socially. I've been to a Look Sussex event with Lucy. We made pizzas and it was simply inspiring to see these great kids enjoying doing something that they might not otherwise get the chance to do.

So, here's a local charity, close to my heart, focused on visually impaired children, creating life experiences and providing a support network for their parents and siblings too. It's a no-brainer. I have also decided to set myself a £1,000 target.

22 February

It was my turn to write a team blog at work this week. It can be a good way of sharing what's going on, keeping people informed, an opportunity to thank or single out some people for good work and to add a bit of flavour from what's going on in our personal lives, just to prove we're human. It was also a great opportunity to announce my fundraising.

My training has been going well. I've lost seven pounds since Christmas and I've already started to notice the difference in feeling a little lighter on my feet. The only issue is I still have trouble with my foot, plus I seem to have picked up a shoulder injury, as I can't move my arm above shoulder height. I've been to the doc's this week and she's referred me for physiotherapy. The good news is I've been advised to see someone who has treated me before using acupuncture and it worked a treat then. I really hope it does this time.

I published my blog at work and created my fundraising page. I also linked it to my Facebook profile. It was approaching half past four and Stu and I had another walk planned. This time we were both working from home, so we decided we'd walk to a town six miles away, have a bite to eat with a mandatory glass of wine (having done more research this is apparently like being on the Camino, and we want our training to be as genuine and realistic as possible), and return.

When I got back home at 10 pm Lisa greeted me excitedly; apparently since I'd left the house some of my friends had donated and I was already at 31% of my fundraising target.

I'm blown away. I can't believe it. How incredible is that? When people say things like 'your sponsorship is inspiring and will help motivate me through my challenge' I now know exactly how they feel. I'm so glad I decided to do the fundraising. This *will* make a difference.

And, just to prove that something's going on, I received a donation of £100 from Bobby, an old school friend. We left school in 1988 and we both went our separate ways. We reconnected years later on Facebook; Bobby was living in Nottingham at the time and I was in Oxfordshire. By chance, I had a work trip to Nottingham lined up, so we met up at what I am sure was his uncle's Indian restaurant because we were treated like royalty. We had a great evening and we've stayed in touch, albeit only via Facebook. In summary, we've met once in the last thirty-one years, yet he's just been so generous. What's more, the words he left me on the website were very touching and genuinely brought a tear to my eye.

3 March: The Brooksteed Alehouse

Today Lisa and I walked into town to our local outdoor shop, intent on spending some of the vouchers and money I still had left from Christmas, zip-off walking trousers being top of the list.

On our way into town we pass our fantastic local: the Brooksteed

Alehouse, a warm and cosy micro-pub with a brilliant community feel, run by two great guys, John and Aaron. Whilst we were helping ourselves to the free Sunday cheeseboard we got chatting about my training. I say 'free'; punters are expected to make a small donation to charity.

John offered to run the Sunday cheeseboard for Look Sussex, and not just for one Sunday, but every Sunday in May whilst I'm away. Lisa also agreed with John to supplement the cheeseboard with a few homemade tapas dishes on Sunday 12 May. There are two bank holidays in May when the pub is extra busy, so I'm thrilled with this. Is there something going on, or is it that John and Aaron are simply the best landlords in Sussex?

When we got back, with slightly more bags and purchases than I'd gone out for, Lisa told her sister Cara all about the support from the Brooksteed. The upshot of all of this is that on 12 May Lucy, along with some of the other Look Sussex children, is also planning on attending.

10 March

I'm about to break the £1,000 barrier. Fantastic. I have six weeks to go. So I've increased my target to £2,000.

April

Training has been going well. Acupuncture on my foot is helping and the fundraising is still rising. I'm now at £1,350, and on top of all this our local newspaper, the *Worthing Herald*, ran a short article on me.

Work has been really busy recently, but amongst all the craziness I hosted a conference in London for the International Compliance Association. I'm a Fellow member, something I do to keep up my professional knowledge, and this year I offered to facilitate their annual global compliance conference. It was a great day, and by chance (or divine intervention) the keynote speaker was Jason Fox from the TV show *SAS: Who Dares Wins*. I hosted Jason for about thirty minutes over lunch, so it would have been silly not to ask him for some advice about how to prevent and treat blisters. I added his advice to my kit list.

Not long until I leave now, and I've had some great send-off parties at work too. My team arranged an escape room in London, my local office in

Solo 500-mile pilgrimage is more than 'a midlife crisis'

Elaine Hammond
news@worthingherald.co.uk
1903282378

Bank boss Simon Donlevy will be trekking nearly 500 miles on a solo pilgrimage during a six-month sabbatical from the city.

The Worthing father-of-two has always wanted to walk the Camino de Santiago, from St Jean in France to Santiago in Spain.

He will be going the distance on his own, with his rucksack on his back.

Simon said: "It's not your usual midlife crisis, I grant you. No fast car purchase going on here, quite the opposite in fact.

"The idea is it is a pilgrimage that you do on your own. I have always wanted to do this. It is a long way and a long time on my own but I am pretty confident I will make friends."

Simon, 49, will be raising money for Look Sussex, a charity close to his heart,

Simon Donlevy with Lucy and Cara Croke at Brooksteed Alehouse

having helped his visually-impaired niece, Lucy.

The plan is to start the journey on May 3 and finish in Santiago on June 8, the day before his 29th wedding anniversary. Simon will speak to his wife Lisa every day and she will be flying out to meet him at the end.

Simon, head of compliance at Lloyds Bank, said: "I will be getting the early train, the one I usually get to work in London with all my mates,

but they will get off at London Bridge and I will go on to St Pancras International for the Eurostar to France.

"Making the journey by train is all part of it."

He has booked accommodation for the first two nights only and will take the rest as it comes.

He added: "It is completely up to me. There are lots of youth hostels. I will need to walk 15 miles a day, with no rest days."

Brooksteed Alehouse, in South Farm Road, is showing its support by raising money for Look Sussex through its Sunday cheeseboard during May. There will be a Spanish theme on May 12, when Lisa will provide tapas and Lucy will be there with others from Look Sussex to help raise awareness.

Lucy, 12, was born with coloboma, which her mum Cara Croke described as cleft palate of the eye.

Cara said: "Because she doesn't wear glasses, people don't always realise she has sight problems."

The family became involved with Look Sussex about four years ago and Cara is now a trustee.

She said: "It has changed my life, and Lucy's. It is a very small charity but it helps a lot of people. It totally includes the siblings, which is the main thing."

Visit www.justgiving.com/fundraising/simon-donlevy to make a donation.

Hove took me out for a drink and meal, the Midge Ure club organised a get-together in London, and my boss came over to see me on my penultimate day to buy me a drink.

On my last afternoon my previous boss, Alasdair, who'd initially approved my sabbatical, took me for a send-off drink as well. It had gone full circle; it was touching and appreciated. Plus he took me to Fortnum's.

CHAPTER FOUR

Sabbatical Starts

Sunday: Less than one week to the walk

My first day off work is tomorrow and I popped in to see my nieces, Lucy and Ella. Straight away, Lucy was in there: 'Can you pick me up from school tomorrow?' She never misses a trick.

It's lovely that she asked, but really, my first day off: the first day when I'm not owned by a clock! We compromised on me collecting her on Tuesday instead; I couldn't really say no, nor would I want to. I love any time I get with those two.

Monday: Four days until I leave for Santiago

My first Monday morning without having to go to work and it felt brilliant, lying in bed, knowing it was the first of many. Being determined not to just sit about and waste it away, I had a list of self-imposed jobs to do to keep me busy. I was determined to have a coffee and breakfast in my kitchen and look out into the garden, to take time and soak it up, which I did, but as soon as I'd finished I never sat down again.

I turned my attention to things I'd be doing after the Camino; after all, this is a six-month break, not just a five-week walk. I had an exciting time ahead of me with some wonderful things planned, but equally important was making sure that I had plenty of time when I had nothing planned. This was intentional, but not so that I could sit about doing nothing; far from it. The free time was for me to fill with whatever I wanted to do, having had some headspace for five weeks. Time on the trail might let me realise a few things about myself, and I might discover new ventures or things I want to do with the rest of my sabbatical. Failing that, I could always go out on my bike in any downtime. I'm never unhappy doing that.

Despite planning to live as a tramp for the next few weeks, I suddenly realised that the week after I get back, in stark contrast, I have an event to attend that requires a top hat and tails. I urgently needed to rearrange my day to sort suit hire for my return.

The guy in the hire shop did all his handiwork with the tape measure and started entering the details into his computer. You should have seen the cynical look on his face after I asked, 'Could you knock two inches off the waistline, please?' Clearly he thought I was delusional. The date of hire was only just over six weeks hence, but I was convinced, or at least hopeful, that I might end up losing some weight in the intervening period. He wasn't. He made me sign a disclaimer to that effect!

I had such a productive day, ending with me having to rush dinner (I was determined to have it ready for when Lisa came home from work), wolfing it down and rushing to my last Spanish lesson; some things never change, eh?

Lisa got me a scallop shell, the internationally recognised sign of a pilgrim. I even painted a little red cross of St James on it before tying it onto my backpack with dental floss. Yes, dental floss; it is really strong and so much lighter than string. Every gram matters.

Tuesday: Three days to go

I'm feeling a bit in limbo.

I laid all my kit out on the floor yesterday and then started shedding things that I didn't really need, just to keep the weight down. I was quite strict with myself and I felt really pleased with the outcome. I even went to the trouble of cutting out unnecessary pages from my guidebook. Neil suggested that I might want to tear out the pages as each day passes too. There'll be something quite cathartic about doing this, I'm sure.

I got so carried away I nearly forgot about picking Lucy up from school and found myself rushing again! I need time to adapt, clearly.

My worldly possessions for five weeks

Wednesday: Two days to go

Sod's law dictates that whenever I'm going away from home, there's a mini drama to deal with. Today's is a leak coming up from underneath my drive. It will need digging up, locating, repairing and hopefully being relaid so it doesn't look awful.

I got up early again to get on with my jobs, and top of the list now is calling Southern Water. I also need to see John at the Brooksteed later, to take him the Look Sussex collecting tin for my fundraising, plus Stu has invited me over, to see me before I go. The next time we meet will be near León, with only two weeks of walking left – hopefully.

I had a glance at the weather forecast for Friday, and it looks so grim I've decided it might make sense to add a poncho to my kit, just to be *extra* waterproof. I'm going into town today to buy it. I could walk in, but I'm going to save my legs and drive.

I keep asking myself if I have enough kit. Just my subconscious niggling away at me with silly questions like, *Why don't you take a pencil sharpener? They're only light.* A pencil sharpener! Really?

I'm a rapid shopper. Ordinarily I'd have popped into town this morning, whizzed into the shops I needed to visit, bought the items I needed and then returned home. Not today. I find myself killing time a bit, not because I'm bored; it's just the anticipation and apprehension manifesting itself in a very strange way. Maybe I am slowly adjusting to my new pace of life too.

I just received notification of another £70 for the fundraiser from two colleagues at work. I have made a conscious effort to send a personal thank-you note to everyone who has donated so far, so I went to do the same for them.

I can't log on. My work account has been suspended! It's quite a moment.

For years I've had the pressure of knowing that whenever I take a holiday, emails will be piling up, like a little welcome present for when I return to work. This is different, very different; I simply don't exist at work. You'd think that would be a brilliant feeling, but this is taking a while to adjust to. I guess old habits die hard.

The great news, though, is I'm now only £250 away from a new £3,000 target for Look Sussex. Yes, I've put it up again, having smashed through the £2,000 target!

I decided to take a photo of the soles of my shoes today too, on the basis that, if I remember, I could have a 'before and after' comparison. That's assuming I keep them; I might end up throwing them away in disgust at some point.

When I picked Lucy up from school last night it was such a lovely afternoon that I treated her to an ice cream on the beach. It was lovely, and as I was walking with her on the pebbles I made sure I took a moment to reflect on the importance of moments like this, to remember them. After all, I've never been able to do this before.

At that point, Neil video-called me from his Camino Porto: a pilgrimage to Santiago, but this route starts from Portugal. He was acting as lead guide, helping some local friends to achieve their lifelong ambition, drawing upon his advice and experience. I had a quick chat with his latest Camino family and he also spoke with Lucy.

I've told you he's joining me on day eight of my Camino for a few days with Bruce and Jay. What I haven't said is that once Neil gets into Santiago, he'll spend a few days there, and rather than fly back home to Wales he's flying to Madrid to meet Jay, who is arriving from Heathrow, and Bruce, from Gatwick. They all rendezvous within about two hours of each other and they then make their merry way to meet with me in northern Spain, wherever I happen to be. True friendship.

Lisa surprised me. The fact that I took Lucy to the beach gave her more time than she'd bargained for to decorate the porch and house with good-luck balloons and banners, and when I walked into the house a mini banquet was awaiting me. Apparently I had fifteen minutes until people started arriving.

It was such a heartwarming evening, full of love and friendship. I received some wonderful gifts and good-luck cards with beautiful and poignant messages. I don't do cards – I hate them, in fact, as I think they are a waste of money – but what was written in them meant such a lot; I was feeling myself well up at reading our very close friends Steffie and Peter's words.

Then I opened Lisa's card. I simply had to give her a huge hug as her words succeeded in bringing tears to my eyes. She'd also written some lovely quotes inside the front:

'Everywhere is within walking distance, if you have the time' 'Nothing adventured, nothing attained' 'Walking is a man's best medicine' 'Walk with the sun until your shadow disappears' 'Jobs fill your pockets but adventures fill your soul' 'The only impossible journey is the one you never begin' 'You are not a human being on a spiritual journey, but a spiritual being on a human journey'	To my Si I will miss you loads but I know I will be in your heart. Remember it's your road, and yours alone. Others may walk it with you but no one can walk it for you. Relish every moment & I'll see you in Santiago. Buen Camino Lisa xxxx

Thursday: I leave tomorrow

I woke this morning to a lovely little video message from Lucy wishing me luck and telling me how much she loved me. The innocence of youth. I played it to Lisa and we just smiled at each other. At least I'll have it with me on the walk should I need a pick-me-up.

I need to buy a new pair of jeans, but not for the walk! Something I have to do before I leave tomorrow is pack for when Lisa and I hopefully meet up again in Santiago. She's going to bring some clean clothes out for me.

A quick trip to the shops shouldn't take too much time on my last day, or so I thought. I kept receiving calls from people wishing me luck. I embraced and enjoyed them all. Normally I'd be rushing to get on with the next thing, but this is my time, so I used it to listen properly and savour the intent. It felt good.

First was a call from Charlotte at work, wanting to update me on a few funny events. Bruce called to say how much he is looking forward to meeting me at the end of next week. It felt strange when he said that, as it still feels like that's weeks away, so it gave me a good thought to cling onto. And then Martyn called; of course he did. I know he's gutted that he can't come out with Neil, Jay and Bruce.

Martyn is an awesome friend, my best friend; he'd do absolutely anything and everything for me, or Lisa, and I love him for it. The simple fact of the matter is he works so damned hard, finding the time to meet up was always going to be a challenge. I fully understand why he can't come, but I know he will be there with me.

He has two great kids, Toby and Zara, and he wanted to know the route so that they could track my progress each day. I explained how to do that through the app I'm using called Polarsteps. I can just see him now, showing them and explaining what their crazy uncle (with a small 'u') Simon is doing in Spain.

The sun is still shining today in the UK, but the forecast for France on Friday is still rain. My foot hasn't properly healed (no pun intended), so I've accepted that it is just going to hurt. I just hope it doesn't ruin it for me. There's only one way to find out, I guess.

The good news is the leak under my driveway has been fixed.

I think I'm ready.

PART 2

The Walk

CHAPTER FIVE

A Pilgrimage Starts at One's Own Front Door

Day 0: En route to St Jean

Five forty-five in the morning. I knew it would be a difficult farewell with Lisa, but my mood was changed the moment I stepped out of our front door. I could hear a small child puffing and panting and getting nearer. I was initially concerned, and then Ella appeared, in her slippers and pyjamas, with a beaming smile. She was out of breath from running down the street. Lucy followed, along with Cara and Chris, all running because they were worried they'd missed me. I just laughed at them, all standing in their pyjamas and dressing gowns, and gave them all a great big hug. Lisa hadn't told me they were coming and it was just the tonic to lighten my departure.

I walked down the street to Worthing station, not wanting to look back, but I did; I couldn't resist one last glance and waved back up the street to the Crokes and Lisa. I turned back. Here I go: my first few kilometres.

I sat on the City Thameslink train to London St Pancras, and I started to shake. This wasn't due to the dreadfully uncomfortable seats, the lack of a table to put a drink on, or the awful sterile interior that looked like a hospital waiting room; I am, after all, used to that through commuting. It was very weird and I hadn't experienced it before. It wasn't just my hands shaking either. I was shivering, like I was cold at the core, but I wasn't cold; it was May and was quite warm. It was fear, I think, coupled with the emotion of leaving Lisa. Some chemical was coursing through my veins and I didn't like it. Thankfully it stopped after about fifteen minutes.

Cara, Lucy and Ella: a surprise early morning send-off party!

The Eurostar terminal was rammed, primarily as it was the Friday before the early May bank holiday. People were queuing all the way out onto the concourse, so I politely joined the end of the line.

I then felt a tap on my shoulder; it was Jo, one of Lisa's best friends from school. She smiled, gave me a hug over one of those ropes like the ones you find outside a nightclub, and said, 'Follow me.'

Jo deals with the VIPs on Eurostar; let's just say she's on first-name terms with David and Victoria and leave it at that. I got given the right royal treatment and before I knew it I was through security, sitting in a lounge with upgraded tickets. Friends in high places, eh?

As I walked along the platform my brother Rich called me, told me how proud he was of me and that he loved me. I was blown away. I'm not even on the Camino yet and there's already something going on. He's never told me that.

I found my seat, was presented with a glass of champagne and ordered my hot breakfast. I have to admit I wasn't your typical-looking business-class customer, dressed in walking trousers, boots and backpack. Equally, this was a million miles away from the taste of life I was about to encounter, but I gratefully accepted it.

I relaxed into the reclining chair and collected my thoughts, smiling as I thought back over the conversation I'd just had with Rich. I wanted to tell Lisa about it, and it started to dawn on me that I was now alone, and it would be that way for some time, with nobody to share any of my new experiences with.

A member of Eurostar staff walked past and noticed my scallop shell on my backpack. It transpires she's Spanish and walked part of the Camino from Burgos to León last year. We chatted for a while and then, just before she went about her business, she told me I'd find it a magical experience.

I have a long day ahead of me: this, my second train already, to Paris Gare du Nord, then across the city via the metro to Montparnasse. I then get a train to Bayonne, and finally onward to St Jean Pied de Port. If all goes well, I should be in St Jean by 10.10 pm. I've booked a B&B for tonight, and shortly after I did so the owner contacted me offering to pick me up from the station. Amazing. Well, he was called Christian!

Given my early start, I decided a nap wasn't out of the question.

I woke on the outskirts of Paris with an idea. Given my next train wasn't for two hours, I could go and make the most of my time in Paris. I love Paris. It is, in my opinion, the most romantic city in the world.

Where should I go? I considered this until the answer became crystal clear. Only last week, an awful fire had swept through and destroyed much of Notre-Dame cathedral, so, given I was on a pilgrimage, there seemed no more fitting place to go and pay homage.

My thoughts were disturbed by a text from Mum. She meant well, but I could tell that she was still very worried, so I called her to stop her worrying about me, again. Lisa is driving to the Midlands tomorrow to help Mum with a car boot sale, so I know that will reassure her.

As I left the train and began to make my way down the platform at Gare du Nord station I heard someone shout, 'Buen Camino.' I turned around and caught the eye of the Spanish girl who'd spoken with me on board, and we exchanged a smile. I sent a 'muchas gracias' her way and walked off thinking that's my first 'buen Camino' of the trip. It's a phrase I'll hear and use a lot over the coming weeks.

Notre-Dame was solemn. In a way it felt like it had become even more of a tourist attraction than it was before the fire. There were gendarmes everywhere, keeping the public away from the ruins. It was sad. I remembered being there before; it had dominated the skyline of the central region of Paris, and now it took some finding.

The train to Bayonne was equally rammed, only this time it was double-decker full. I'd reserved a seat on the top deck, so I was afforded some lovely views of the French countryside, albeit ones we were whizzing past well in excess of 100 miles per hour. If only the trains in the UK were this fast.

As I gazed out the window, I settled back into my seat. I made the most of it, particularly as I realised that it was probably the most comfortable seat I'd be sitting in for the foreseeable future.

Bayonne itself was beautiful, a quaint Basque town formed at the point where three rivers meet. I found a little restaurant, which was more of a newsagent's with a few tables in it and tried to understand the menu. My French is OK, obviously my Spanish is beginner's level, but Basque? It was all X's and Z's. I ordered what I thought was a burger but ended up eating a fried steak hash with salad and fries. It was quite good, though, and helped me pass the time until I needed to get back to Bayonne station.

I sat on a bench on the platform. After five minutes I realised that my train was already here, some thirty minutes before departure, just sitting at one end of the platform. The giveaway sign was seeing a few people get on with backpacks. I picked up mine and climbed aboard.

Normally, when you get on a train, nobody speaks. Not so here. We were all instant friends. I sat at a table for four and was instantly joined by Thiago from Brazil, in his mid-twenties, Antonio from Italy, about sixty-five years I'd guess, and Eddie from South Korea. Greg and Kim, brother and sister from Oregon, USA, moved seats to come and sit with us at the table opposite.

Antonio spoke no English, and he was the centre of attention. Thankfully Thiago spoke Italian and translated, which was useful as we were all trying to understand why Antonio was taking the contents out of his rather large and heavy-looking backpack and scattering them all over the table, huffing and shaking his head as he did so. Thiago explained that Antonio had been ill, to the point where he nearly hadn't made the trip at all, but when he had woken up this morning he'd felt better, so his wife had put him on the plane.

Apparently his wife had also packed for him! He had no idea what was inside his backpack, so this was the first time he was seeing everything.

It made me feel good. If ever I had worries about being unprepared, Antonio banished them into oblivion. His wife clearly had no idea what was involved; she had, after all, packed him two pairs of jeans, plus he was already wearing one pair. We all laughed as the contents kept coming out.

As we left the train, the guard started shouting after him, 'Monsieur, monsieur,' and pointed to Antonio's belongings piled up on the table. Antonio, with an air of reluctant acceptance, just raised a hand, as if to say, *Sorry, I can't carry them, you have them,* and we all left, laughing. Where else would this happen? People of different nationalities, who don't speak the same language, enter a train as strangers and one hour later leave as friends.

Christian was waiting for me, as promised. He pointed my new friends in the direction of accommodation, and then took me to his B&B. Only he didn't. He took me on a tour of St Jean. He gave me a complete orientation to the town so that I would know exactly where to go in the morning. He pointed out the start, the pilgrim's office, the gates as you exit the city, and then drove up a steep hill – the foothills of the Pyrenees, in fact – to show me where I might go wrong tomorrow. He didn't want me to accidentally take the less attractive lower route to Roncesvalles, which is, apparently, easily done. What a welcome.

We got back to the B&B and he offered to make me a hot drink, but I was so tired I politely declined and got my head down. I have to be completely honest; I lay in my bed completely shitting myself about what I was about to embark upon.

Day 1: St Jean Pied de Port to Orisson

I woke to sheep standing in a steep field outside my window: sodden sheep, owing to the rain. I couldn't see the top of the field as very low clouds hung in the air. Every day there are people starting the Camino from St Jean, they've been doing it for hundreds of years, and today I would be another.

I was very excited when I met Christian at breakfast. He was so jolly and seemed genuinely excited for me too; it was like I was the first pilgrim to ever leave his B&B. It transpired he used to work in the UK and established Fish!

Kitchen, a great restaurant in Borough Market that Lisa and I have been to; small world.

I went back to my room and carefully checked I had everything in my backpack, and hauled it on, feeling excited, yet apprehensive about what lay ahead. All that planning and training was about to come into its own, hopefully.

I went back downstairs and Christian, who seemed more excited than I was, asked if he could take some photographs of me leaving his B&B. Maybe he wanted to use them on his website, I thought. He'd been such a fantastic host I was happy to go along with it.

After the final photo I waved a final farewell at Christian, who shouted after me, 'Buen Camino, and may the Lord be with you.' As he did this, I suddenly realised today was Star Wars Day, and I hadn't considered that before. 'May the fourth be with me,' I uttered to myself with a smile, walking through the archway that officially marks the beginning of the Camino. I had a real spring in my step.

St Jean was peaceful and quaint. Every pilgrim has to register at the pilgrim's office, a small tourist-looking shop that's easy to miss on the narrow cobbled streets. They were very helpful. They also made me complete questionnaires about why I was walking the Camino, and then I had to weigh my backpack. I had already heard them telling some people that their bags were too heavy and that they needed to shed some weight. Thankfully, when they hung my bag on the big hook under the scales, my backpack was within the maximum for my height by about six kilos. I'd passed the first pilgrim test – happy days.

I was then handed all sorts of papers, the most important of which seemed to be the huge list of albergues along the route. I tucked this one safely in a zipped pocket in my bag. I ditched the rest as needless weight.

As I left the town and walked the first kilometre I wondered what the hell I had taken on. It was so damned steep. It was on tarmac too, just a road, but bloody hell! Thankfully after another two kilometres it turned into a gentler gradient, and then the Pyrenees revealed the most beautiful green and mountainous landscape. I breathed it in. It was, however, still up, and up some more, to the point where when I finally arrived at my accommodation I called Stu and my opening words to him were 'Fuck me, that was steep!' He bellowed with laughter.

On the way, I passed a lady from California called Luna. She kept stopping to smell the lavender and other flowers. She's seventy-two, the same age as my mum, alone and enjoying life to the full. I walked with her for about twenty minutes, and then she went off to check the aroma of another bud and told me to walk ahead, wishing me a friendly 'buen Camino'.

I'm so glad that when I met Søs before Christmas she recommended I stay in Refuge Orisson. It is about two thirds of the way up and is a pretty little place with the most stunning views.

I did some wine yoga with Kat, a Tasmanian girl, and Karen, her mum, looking over the mountains. I asked what wine yoga was all about and was told, in a broad Aussie accent, 'Wine yoga is stretching with a glass of wine, silly!' Kat elaborated, 'For example, you have to put your wine on the floor, put your leg up on a rail, stretch down to retrieve the receptacle, take a swig, then return it to the floor. You then repeat in different poses.' I don't suppose it would take off at your local gym, but it worked a treat out here, and it was nice to have some light-hearted fun too.

Limbering up for 'wine yoga' in the Pyrenees

I then showered using the one token I was given when I checked in. I had no idea how long the water would last with the token and I didn't want to run out of water with soap on me, so it was a very rapid shower!

As I stepped out of the tiny cubicle, I unfortunately timed my exit to coincide with a group of passing pilgrims who had also just checked in, and they were all female. I found myself rapidly fumbling for my travel towel, offering an 'Oops, excuse me, I didn't realise that this towel doesn't wrap all the way around me!'

I also did some clothes washing by hand, for the first time – ever! This is when I realised that I had forgotten to bring something with me: a peg. It is only day one, so I've started wondering what else I might have forgotten to include in my kit.

Some people had carefully hung their wet laundry secured to a line. I placed mine gingerly in a corner, hoping that it wouldn't blow away, because if it did it would probably blow about a kilometre down a steep valley.

After about an hour I decided that the weight of my clothes would be less, given they would now be drier, and I didn't want to risk leaving them there any longer; it's not like I could just pop to a shop tomorrow morning and replace my whole wardrobe if it got blown away. And there it was: a lonely, unused peg. It secured my washing a treat. Yes, one peg gripped all my clothes as securely as I could muster.

Afterwards, once the clothes were dry, I decided that the peg might come in handy on future days. I don't like to think of it as theft; more that the Camino provided when I most needed it.

Dinner that night was a real eye-opener and a stark reminder that some people are walking this thing for some very different and more real reasons than mine. After being served a wonderful communal Camino family meal, all forty-two of us were encouraged to keep the tradition of the refuge. We had to stand up, one by one, introduce ourselves and explain why we were walking the Camino.

Our host said, 'It doesn't matter if you don't yet know your reasons; just be honest with yourself and your fellow pilgrims.'

Wow. The first thing I noticed was the true international feel to the room. We had pilgrims from Brazil, Canada, Australia, Thailand, Philippines, Taiwan and South Korea, to name a few.

And oh, how the stories struck a chord. A guy from Brazil was involved in a motorcycle accident five years ago and broke every bone in his body. Walking the Camino was the goal he had set himself during his rehabilitation. There was a quiet lady with cancer who played down the fact that she only had a few months left to live. One guy was walking it simply because he said he could.

A US citizen from Trinidad called Chris explained that his wife had died a couple of years ago and he was here because of her. I felt a connection with him more than anyone. I'm not sure why, and we didn't speak to each other until we retired to our dorms, where we just shook hands and exchanged an understanding glance. A few moments later we shared our first laugh together too, because looking around my bedroom I noticed there were eight bunks, seven of them being occupied by women. He was in the room next door, with exactly the same ratio!

We all spent some time working out shifts for charging our mobile phones and started to retire for the day. At least tomorrow, once I've crested, it should be more downhill.

I lay on my top bunk reflecting upon my current situation. I'm determined to spend more time in the here and now on this walk, as opposed to continually planning ahead for the next thing, driven by a calendar both at work and at home. Here I am, halfway up the Pyrenees, in a room with seven strange women. Some have already fallen asleep, the giveaway sign being a low drum of snoring. It isn't too loud, though, and my earplugs shouldn't have any trouble blocking it out.

I thought about the lows and highs. I don't think I've had a 'low' today; I've enjoyed every minute. My euphoric moment was, however, finding the peg. The Camino is already stripping me back to basics.

My thoughts drifted back to dinner, to what I'd told my fellow pilgrims were my reasons for walking the Camino. 'I've worked for thirty-one years and decided I deserve some "me time" and some space to breathe. I've taken a sabbatical for six months, and this is only day six. I am approaching the Camino with an open mind, to let it talk to me.'

I'd kept it simple. It was honest, but I didn't go into the fact that it also felt like a calling, having experienced a small part of it before. Maybe that was the whole purpose of the exercise, to get pilgrims to really consider their reasons for being here, having walked for one day. I wondered if everyone else was thinking about what they'd said. Well, the ones who were awake, anyway.

I don't remember joining the others in the land of nod.

Day 2: Orisson to Roncesvalles

Fog was swirling around the mountains, creating a haunting atmosphere. It was also very cold, and the refuge owners told me it had dropped to minus 15°C overnight.

The refuge made lunches on request, and, given there were no shops between here and Roncesvalles, it was an easy decision. I picked mine up after breakfast.

I packed my bag. I've never spent so long checking and double-checking I have everything. Everyone was doing the same. I presume I'll get into some routine over the coming days, but the one thing you don't practise in training is how and where to pack everything so you know you haven't forgotten anything. The last thing I want to do is walk twenty kilometres and realise I've left something behind.

It was still cold when I set out. In fact, it was freezing. The wind chill was -8°C, but on the flip side I was treated to one of nature's most incredible phenomena: an air frost. Anything with moisture on (leaves on trees, long blades of grass) looked ice-blasted, to the point where for about ten kilometres it was like walking through a winter wonderland. It was amazing, and, once the fog lifted, the ice-white trees were juxtaposed against a backdrop of lush green fields and a stunning blue sky. It was a photographer's paradise.

To top all that I spotted a couple of condors soaring above me, swooping in and out of the mist. They were huge but graceful birds of prey and I just stood for a while watching them gliding effortlessly on the mountain wind.

I found myself walking with a group of people, including Chris and Luna. I later realised that I was walking with some of Chris's dorm from last night; he was the only bloke and I had gatecrashed his harem.

Ami, Clare and Laurel were all friends from Devon. Rather embarrassingly they reminded me about when we first met, last night, just as I got out the shower! They were only walking for one week, to Pamplona. Laurel had walked from Pamplona to Santiago before, so she was here to

complete the leg from St Jean to Pamplona. Ami just loved walking and was here with her friends. Clare was an Irish lady who had an uncanny knack of just making you laugh. I really liked them, and spent the day with them chatting and walking.

Laurel, who is a keen gardener, told me she had recently been working on the late Christopher Robin's garden. I guess with a name like that it was probably her destiny.

We stopped for a drink where a guy had set up a van just before the exposed pass at the top. The van provided some much-needed shelter from the bitterly cold wind and consequently he was doing a roaring trade.

Chris and I noticed an American lady with no gloves and she looked really unwell. She'd been separated from her friends; they'd gone ahead and she had no money, so I bought her a hot chocolate and she tried to defrost her hands on the cup. When Chris suggested she put walking socks over her hands, her face lit up at the simple but brilliant idea. It took her a while to get her fingers to work and open the buckles on her backpack.

I thought downhill would be easier. Oh, how wrong I was. However, as we rounded a corner we found Clare, sitting cross-legged on a rock with her woolly hat tilted to one side, singing a ditty, which went something like 'I'm a little leprechaun and I've found a pot of gold'. She had us all in stitches and it really lightened the load.

We found a spot on the descent that was slightly sheltered from the bitterly cold wind and ate our frozen sandwiches.

There was a long line of pilgrims waiting to check in at the massive monastery in Roncesvalles. It can cater for about 180 pilgrims. Having slogged up and over the Pyrenees my legs were knackered and I just wanted a shower and a lie down on a mattress. I guess everyone was the same, but in true pilgrim style we all waited patiently.

One of the Dutch hospitaleros (yes, this huge monastery, which officially marks the start of the Camino for the Spanish, is for some reason run by the Dutch confraternity) walked down the line counting heads; he stopped after he got to Chris and me. He then told the others behind Chris that the monastery was full and they would have to find somewhere else to stay. We were lucky. There was a Swedish girl behind Chris who then started to have a panic, so Chris kindly let her have his place and he left to get a taxi to

Frozen sandwiches!

another village nearby, assuming there was one. I grabbed his number so we could try to hook up in the morning.

Check-in was overcomplicated, with lots of form filling, and explained the long line outside the office. The dormitory, despite being the biggest room I've ever slept in, was well laid out and the bed was pretty comfortable. The shower felt incredible.

I decided to go to mass before dinner: not something I've ever willingly done before. It was peaceful. The priest read out the nationalities of everyone staying in the monastery tonight. It must have taken two full minutes for him to complete the list of countries – wow. He then called all the pilgrims to the front to receive a blessing, so I duly joined in. I'm not Catholic and know I can't receive communion, but this was just a blessing, so I didn't feel like a fraud. Anyhow, I figured I should take whatever help is on offer, even if it is divine support.

Then something totally unexpected happened. The American whose hands had nearly dropped off on the mountain sidled up against me to thank me for the hot chocolate. I received my blessing from the priest and walked back to my pew. As I did, I began to stroke the first few bristles of my new beard. The American, who was still walking alongside me, looked at my hand and said, 'Ah, look at you, you're married and everything, *and* I really liked you as well!'

I didn't know what to say or do, other than try to make a quick exit as soon as mass finished. I could have sworn she was with a husband at the albergue last night. She asked me to go for a drink. I politely declined and left as quickly as my tired legs would take me. Of all the places.

We were all scheduled to have pilgrim meals in shifts, at various restaurants around the monastery, so I headed to where mine was located. En route, I thankfully bumped into Clare, Ami, Luna and Laurel. I told them about what had happened in mass, much to their amusement, and they invited me to join them at dinner. I felt safer in their company.

Day 3: Roncesvalles to Zubiri

Have I died? I can hear chanting from Gregorian monks. I have never been so happy to open my eyes. It's not like there was a little welcome pack lying on my bunk that explained at 6 am I'd be woken by the sound of Gregorian monks chanting throughout the monastery. Once I'd got over the shock of being woken from a very deep sleep in this way I lay in bed welcoming it, smiling; it was quite calming, really.

I became more aware of my surroundings and realised I had my first decision of the day to make. Do I get out of bed first and expose my body to the elderly Spanish couple sleeping in the bunks opposite me, or do I let them go first? She was no looker, so I got up!

I called Chris. He was in a place called Erro and according to my map he was six kilometres ahead of me.

We set off through a beautiful forest. I left the girls to walk behind me: not far behind, but far enough that I could have some solitude and listen to the beautiful birdsong in silence.

It was good to see Chris. He was disappointed that he hadn't stayed in Roncesvalles, but on the flip side he was happy to have made a few extra kilometres via a taxi the night before, which gave him more time to sit and sip coffee at a local café. We all met up in the café, had a bite to eat, drank some more coffee and set off.

The walk into Zubiri is a killer: rocky, downhill and on a cliff top where the rock protrudes at an angle so you can't place your feet flat on the floor.

I met a nice guy called Shane and, boy, did he need to talk. That's what the Camino is all about, though; you meet people, complete strangers, and they tell you of their worst nightmares, fears and woes. There's a wonderful innocence about it that allows people to unburden their life history.

This afternoon, it was my turn to listen and, by doing so, help Shane. He explained that his wife was an alcoholic and he'd had enough. Apparently she had returned to the monastery drunk, loud and violent last night. He said he was so embarrassed that he'd given her some money and sent her packing this morning. He told me she was beyond help, that he'd spent a fortune on doctors and medication for her, and he had thought bringing her on the Camino would help.

It was only about thirty minutes into listening to Shane's sorry tale that the penny dropped. Blimey, we're talking about that crazy woman who hit on me in mass last night. I didn't have the heart to tell him, but I was delighted to hear she'd left the Camino.

Shane talked all the way to Zubiri; he needed to, and I was happy to listen and count my blessings. Chris and the girls walked ahead and I lost them in the distance.

When we arrived, Shane couldn't get any accommodation. I had phoned ahead earlier that day. It just seemed so busy, and after people had been turned away from the monastery last night I'd decided it might be best to do this.

We started chatting to some pilgrims already drinking a beer outside a little bar, who told us that Zubiri was full, and they explained why. Apparently for four days before my arrival in St Jean the weather over the Pyrenees had been so bad that they had closed the path. This meant that some people either got a taxi to Roncesvalles and started their Camino from there, walked the lower route, or, as they had done, stayed holed up in St Jean. Hopefully it would thin out a bit as the days passed.

Shane embraced me, thanked me for listening, and we exchanged a 'buen Camino'. He was going to walk on to the next village to find somewhere to sleep.

I walked into my albergue and was met by a smiling young lady. 'Hola! You must be Simon.' I was last to arrive, obviously.

She could see that I was knackered, so she said not to worry about paying or getting my pilgrim's passport stamped yet, and showed me to my bunk. The passport proves I'm a real pilgrim and thus entitles me to the cheap accommodation, though it baffles me that any normal tourist would choose to stay in an albergue whilst on holiday in Northern Spain. It will ultimately serve as my proof of having walked the Camino when I present it at the pilgrim's office in Santiago to collect my compostela, the official certificate.

Obviously arriving last means one thing: a top bunk, and probably the worst one, near the door. I was right. The room seemed full of Germans, apart from a very elderly South Korean lady who was already asleep on my bottom bunk. It was impossible to get onto my bed without shaking the whole rickety frame and waking her, but I needed to lie down before unpacking. I never mind being a shortarse, but when it's the top bunk I can never reach to unpack properly on the bed! I could hear Martyn's voice in my head calling me a munchkin as I gingerly climbed up.

The owner came in with the paperwork. I asked if I could do some washing and she offered to do it for me for €2. I jumped down, went to the bathroom, stripped off, wrapped what I could of my tiny little travel towel around my waist and stepped back out to hand her all my dirty washing – bargain.

Having showered and dressed, I went into a local bar for some food, but was so tired I wasn't feeling very sociable. I then saw a woman looking rather panic-stricken. As she got nearer, I could see it was Shane's wife, desperately looking for him, or her next drink. She clearly hadn't gone home. I knew Shane wasn't in town, but after the events of last night I kept my head down and let her pass.

When I got to the room, everyone was either sleeping or looking at their phones, probably contacting loved ones or looking at tomorrow's route. Surely it wouldn't be as hard as this afternoon's surface.

A German girl asked me if I could turn the lights off. I asked if everyone was now in, and she confirmed that was the case. It fell to me, then. The unwritten rule of albergues: the last one in turns the lights off.

I climbed up into my bunk, in the dark, trying hard not to disturb the Korean lady underneath me sporting full eye mask and earplugs. The sudden swaying of the bed as my body weight moved onto the steel ladder gave her a fright. She peeled the mask away in a hurry as I offered a polite apology through the darkness.

I lay in bed feeling shattered and noticed I'd received an email from Christian, my host in St Jean. He sent me some lovely words of encouragement along with the photographs he'd taken of me outside his B&B when I left on day one. I was feeling a bit low and lonely, and it really picked me up. There's something going on! (#TSGO!)

Or maybe not! Twenty minutes later, when we were all in a state of 'mobile lights out' and tucked up in sleeping bags, a doorbell rang. It kept ringing. Surely someone on a bottom bunk would go to the door. It kept ringing, every thirty seconds or so, but nobody moved. So with a bit of a huff and puff I exclaimed, 'I'll go, then, shall I?' and climbed out of bed, this time not caring one bit about my roommates or the lady below me who was violently awoken by a minor earthquake.

I approached the door in my underpants and wondered what was going to greet me on the other side. Dressed like this, it could be entertaining.

I think I initially gave the guy on the opposite side of the door a little fright. He was also a pilgrim, apparently staying at this albergue, but had forgotten the code to get back in as he arrived after curfew. He was apologetic yet grateful.

At least this meant I could get back into bed with the lights on and leave him to do the honours. I think he realised how much he'd disturbed everyone, because when he returned from the bathroom, he simply hit the lights and slept on his bed fully clothed.

Day 4: Zubiri to Pamplona

Why do people get up so early? It is impossible to creep about at 5 am, zipping up sleeping bags and clicking backpack buckles, without waking your roommates, even with earplugs in – grrr!

I gave up trying to sleep through it, so I climbed out of bed and starting gathering my stuff, and my thoughts: *I've not slept well, but that's par for the course. Try to embrace it, stay calm, and get on with the day.*

I felt a tap on the shoulder; it was the guy from last night. Without hesitation he gave me a hug, and, whilst still holding on to my shoulders, said, 'I can't thank you enough for letting me in last night, and if I see you again the beers are on me.' I was still in my underwear!

It seemed unreal that I would be in our first major city tonight. There were only five on the whole route: Pamplona, Logroño, Burgos, León and Santiago itself.

I met up with Ami, Clare and Laurel and we waited for Chris and Luna to join us. Apparently one of the locals had taken them to a farmhouse up in the hills last night. Ami, Clare and Laurel invited me to stay with them in their rented apartment tonight.

We stopped for some lunch in a shack and Chris recommended I try the chicharrón – fried belly pork. It was delicious, but then disaster struck. A molar broke in half. I'd been toying with having a rest day in Pamplona tomorrow, but now there was no debate. I will need to find a dentist. I only have two rest days built into my schedule if I'm going to reach Santiago by 8 June, and here I am, four days in, needing to use one already. It doesn't bode well.

The start of the Camino is a shock to the system and my guidebook tells me that many of the hospitals and clinics around Pamplona can be full of pilgrims who have set off too hard. Listening to my body, it needs a rest; the Pyrenees and Zubiri weren't easy, so maybe this is a good thing.

We set off together until mid-afternoon, where there was an option built into the route. The others wanted to walk a flatter, meandering route along the riverbanks. I wanted to do the proper Camino route that went up the side of a steep mountain, so we agreed on a meeting point where the two routes joined later and off I set.

It was great. I met a guy who was selling fruit and I think I recognised him from the film *The Way*; we had a chat before I pressed on. I met a lady from Brazil walking with her daughter Gabriella, who coincidentally lives in Putney, where my eldest son lives. I also met another guy from the film in a beautiful little village called Trinidad – a shame that Chris had missed this.

Where the path rejoined the river I found a little café and decided to wait for them. I figured I would have travelled faster as my route, whilst steeper, was definitely shorter. I called Neil, and we had a long chat. I only considered the time as I hung up. Surely they must be here by now?

I called Chris. He said they were lost, that they had wandered away from the river and were now only a couple of kilometres from Pamplona (which he beautifully pronounces 'Pamp-a-lona' in his cool, deep Trinidadian accent). I was at least seven kilometres away, so we agreed I'd meet them at the accommodation.

47

It was a long, lonely and hot slog over the last few kilometres, and I was so tired when I arrived on the outskirts of Pamplona that I could hardly look up. At least I've got a rest day tomorrow, so I can have a proper look around.

I eventually found the apartment and rang the buzzer. Ami came to meet me and offered to carry my backpack. I declined until she told me the apartment was five storeys up and there was no lift. So I reluctantly accepted the help. I was hot, sweaty, dirty and completely shattered.

We showered, made full use of having our own washing machine and went for a pre-dinner drink in the large and bustling plaza in the city. Over much laughter the truth about this afternoon's adventures started to unravel. Ami explained that Chris hadn't actually lied to me when he'd said that they were lost, and it had also been true that they were only a couple of kilometres away from the city. The bit that he had failed to tell me, however, and it was quite an important piece of information, was that they were so lost they had hopped onto a passing bus to Pamplona from about five kilometres out. I'd been had! I no longer felt so guilty about accepting Ami's help up the stairs.

Chris said he'd booked himself into a suite in a posh hotel for two nights. He said, despite the bus journey, he was so tired when he arrived he didn't even enquire about the price! He's offered for me to stay with him tomorrow night.

My bed tonight consists of sofa cushions strategically placed on the floor. I'm sharing the lounge with Luna, who is sleeping on the rest of the sofa. The rest of the girls are in the bedrooms.

Three days ago I didn't know these people. Now we sleep, wash our laundry together and walk around in our underwear as though we've been friends for life. I hung out the washing earlier, handling strangers' knickers without batting an eyelid. The Camino still finds a way to work its magic, stripping me back to basics, even when I'm not staying in an albergue.

I'm pretty comfortable on my makeshift bed, and as I start to close my eyes I comfort myself with the knowledge that at least I'm not going to be woken ridiculously early by the backpack rustlers!

Day 5: Rest day in Pamplona

Sleeping until 8 am was a bit of a bonus. Staying at the apartment means I can leave my backpack here and walk around without any weight on my back in the hunt for a dentist.

I found a busy café in Pamplona and just sat, people-watching. I was enjoying the hustle and bustle but felt like a stranger looking in; I suppose I was.

I had impressed myself with my very basic Spanish, both in the café and when I called in at the dentist earlier. I have to admit I needed to look up a few words; unsurprisingly my beginner's Spanish classes hadn't covered the vocabulary for emergency dentistry. I'm trying to practise where I can, and the locals seem to appreciate the effort, even if they speak a little English.

I looked at my guidebook and worked out I've walked sixty-seven kilometres. There's still some 700 kilometres ahead of me and the good news is I have no blisters yet. I wonder how far I'd walk in total if I included extra things like walking around Pamplona to find a dentist!

I'm killing time, really, waiting for my 1 pm appointment. After the dentist my next priority is to buy a razor; this beard is driving me mad!

*

Spanish dentistry is incredible. The dentist completely rebuilt my molar, I received wonderful care and service, and all for €58. I have dental insurance, so I found a bench and submitted an online claim using my phone. Normally it might take me a few days to get round to doing this, but here I simply had the time.

Tooth mended, razor bought, I decided it was time to become a tourist in Pamplona. I followed a route up to the cathedral, along the same streets where they have the famous 'running of the bulls'. I paid to enter the cathedral (you get a significant discount as a pilgrim) and enjoyed the tranquillity and sheer size of the place. It seemed to go on and on, and was a maze of rooms. In one, an archaeological dig was underway and I could hear someone chipping away below me.

After I'd finished exploring I decided I'd walked enough for a rest day, so I found a little tapas bar in the old town and telephoned Chris. He was with the girls, and they were about to visit the cathedral. I told them it was incredible and to look out for the live dig. They agreed to meet me later in the bar. I figured a couple of hours with a beer might help my tooth subside, and by then I might feel brave enough to eat on it too.

When they arrived Chris told me that I had missed an amazing show. He asked me if I had seen all the goats around the back of the church. I hadn't. He explained that each day, at 3 pm, they recreate the spectacle of the bulls running through the streets of Pamplona, but in order to do it safely with all the children and tourists about, they do it with the goats. He went on, explaining how they had been running along the streets with all these goats. It sounded awesome and I was gutted I'd missed it.

Then Ami laughed, and they all started to giggle, followed by roaring hysterical laughter. The bugger had fooled me again! The 'running of the goats' story would become legendary.

Apparently it all stemmed from the fact that when they were in the cathedral they came across the archaeological dig. The man I heard chiselling away was, according to my new prankster friends, just a recording. So the fact that I had been so gullible gave them an idea to exploit it some more.

I have to take my hat off to Chris, though: in his deadpan Trinidadian accent he was so convincing, plus it was the first time I'd seen the very dry side of his humour. He did it so well. We all laughed about it continually throughout the afternoon (and drank some more beers, of course).

Chris and I really have bonded. He told me a few more things about himself this afternoon as we sat and grazed on tapas (slightly softer tapas than the chicharrón of yesterday). Since his wife, Karen, had died two years ago he had naturally found life different. He told me he had recently given himself a kick up the arse (my words) and decided to do this walk to help himself sort his life out. I sensed it was a big thing for him to confide in me in this way. He explained to me that Karen enjoyed walking but they never did the Camino because they were always working so hard and never really had the time. I knew that feeling, but it made me appreciate even more the decision I had made to take a break from work, to step off the hamster wheel.

Along with his pilgrim's passport, Chris is doing something rather special. He's also brought Karen's actual US passport with him and he's getting that stamped at the albergues too. To him it feels like he's bringing her with him on this amazing journey – just beautiful.

There are so many other stories like this out here. There's a truly international feel too. I'm meeting people from all over the world and everyone is so friendly and supportive. If this could just breed across the planet a little, it would be incredible to be a human on earth. I know, a bit profound, but it's so true. I just love the spirit here.

Chris insisted on me moving into his palatial suite. It was luxurious. We had robes, shower gel and big fluffy white towels. It made me realise how already, in such a short space of time, the Camino had begun to teach me about the basics of life and, more importantly, what we can do without – but they were so fluffy, and look, there are slippers too! At least I won't have to dry my towel by hanging it on the outside of my backpack in the morning.

We all met up in the square for dinner and champagne. Ami and Laurel fly back tomorrow, so we had to give them a decent send-off. Clare was, however, toying with staying on and maybe walking more of the Camino with Luna. Kat and Karen, whom I hadn't seen since wine yoga in Orisson, also joined us. The highlight of the evening, though, was when Chris ordered one of every tapas dish that they had behind the counter. There was a lot! The food just kept coming all evening.

Tomorrow Chris and I will head out to the windmills atop the hills off to the west of Pamplona. Another long day ahead, but hopefully it will feel easier after the rest today.

Day 6: Pamplona to Puente la Reina

We left the comfort of our little palace in the dark, wearing woolly hats to keep the chill off. Looking up at the stars, we knew they wouldn't be needed for long. We followed the shells. Every few metres throughout Pamplona the Camino is marked with metal shells on the ground; they appeared about two kilometres before the city and, this morning, seemed to be with us for another two kilometres. They peter out just as you get a view of the famous landmark of the windmills on the top of the hills just west of the city. It then becomes obvious where to go: up!

We found a little café halfway up and stopped for our newfound mid-morning routine: coffee, freshly squeezed orange juice and a bit of tortilla (Spanish omelette).

I opened an email from the insurance company telling me that my claim has been rejected. Apparently I need to have proof that I received emergency treatment because I was abroad. Ordinarily I would have got irritated, but the Camino was working its magic on me already. So I simply replied explaining my predicament:

Hello

Thanks for your reply. I am a pilgrim walking the Camino de Santiago. My tooth broke 3 days ago and I was waiting to walk to Pamplona to get the treatment, which I did yesterday. Thank God.

Today I have left Pamplona. I am 12km away and walking further so I cannot go back to prove it was an emergency. I can assure you it was and maybe you're aware of the life of a pilgrim, in which case I trust you will assess this case as you see in my best interests. I will leave it with you to decide. I will accept whatever you think is best and appropriate.

Thank you.

Simon

We continued uphill, walking amongst colourful heather, gorse and bracken for about another forty-five minutes, and came across an amazing little stand offering drinks and snacks. It was amazing because there was no owner, just a basket to collect donations. The basket was full of euros. There really is a wonderful spirit here.

We walked up to the famous pilgrim monument and took some photographs. It was from the top of the windmills that I began to see and feel the true beauty of the Camino off to the west. It was green, rolling, peaceful, and it felt like it was embracing me, saying, *Hey, you've done the hard part, now enjoy it.*

Today was going to be our longest day walking so far, at twenty-four kilometres, but we felt good, refreshed from the day's rest. That feeling ended rather abruptly once we started to descend, though. The path was made up of huge, loose cobbles, which made walking downhill painful and treacherous. It was like walking on a seabed.

But when we got to our albergue, the Estrella Guía, we received the most amazing welcome. Chris went to get his pilgrim passport stamped, along with Karen's passport: a ritual I'm now used to. Something magical then happened. I can't explain it, but the host, Chris and I were all in tears within a few minutes.

In summary, the owner flipped the pages of Karen's passport until she got to the page with her photo on it. She then kissed her own hand and placed her hand, with that kiss, on his wife's photo. With her free hand she held on to Chris's hand and started to pray. She then got her phone and played 'Love Is Still the Answer' by Jason Mraz. The words went straight to his heart and he just sobbed. We all did. Natalia, our host, is amazing.

She showed us to our own private room; we were delighted. She kissed us both and then left us to shower. You don't get that at the Ritz! #TSGO!

I lay in bed reading my guidebook and tending to my feet. Still no blisters, but one is trying its best on my little toe, probably due to the descent this afternoon. I informed Chris that we'd completed 110 kilometres. We both agreed it felt good to have broken the 100-kilometre mark. Only 686 kilometres left . . .

And then I noticed a reply from the insurance company:

Dear Simon

Thanks for your email.

On this occasion we shall assess your claim as an emergency.

I am pleased to confirm your claim has now been processed and a payment of £53.47 will be reimbursed to your account. This can take up to 3 – 5 working days to show in your account.

Should you wish to see a breakdown of how your claim was assessed this can be viewed by logging into your account online.

If you have any further queries, please get in touch.

Kind regards

'There's definitely something going on,' I exclaimed, as I read the reply to Chris. There must be if the spirit of the Camino can influence insurance companies to pay out!

Day 7: Puente la Reina to Estella

We said a fond farewell to Natalia and stepped out to the murky morning air. Heavy rain overnight made for very damp conditions, but at least it had now stopped. It gave the midges a treat, but not us! That said, the birds were in full song and the smells were incredible through the moist morning humidity.

For a few days now we've had beautiful poppies lining the route, and they seemed abundantly in bloom this morning, having enjoyed the early morning rain. We stumbled upon a little bit of paradise too; in fact it had a little wooden sign hanging on a post with the hand-painted words 'Paradise under Construction'.

I've decided that today will be an alcohol-free day. I have drunk wine or beer (champagne doesn't count, right?) every day since leaving home, so I decided I needed a day of abstinence.

There was another honesty box scenario at the stall and, would you believe it, there was even a box of red wine; lead me not into temptation. I went for coffee and placed some euros in the tub with the countless other offerings. Somebody told me that, if you don't have money and you need it to survive, you're welcome to take not only food but also money out of the box. That is the way of the Camino. I love it here.

We stayed in Capuchinos Albergue in Estella, did our washing, then had a pilgrim dinner, which, of course, came with wine. I told the hospitalero that I was having a day off wine, and he simply replied with, 'If it was good enough for Jesus then we too should drink it every day on the Camino,' followed by, 'And, after all, don't priests drink it every day too?' He continued pouring. When the Camino provides, you learn to accept it.

Talking of wine, apparently word on the Camino street is that tomorrow morning we pass by the font that provides free red wine to pilgrims. Better still, Neil, Jay and Bruce come out to meet me, and I can't wait to see them tomorrow night.

In my head I have broken my Camino down into four stages. Stage 1: walking alone until Neil, Jay and Bruce come out. Stage 2: walking with them for three days. Stage 3: walking alone again for another week, and Stage 4: when Stu comes out for the final two weeks. It sounds easy when you say it like that, and the truth is you're never alone, plus I have Chris and we're having such a great time

I wonder how Chris is feeling. It must be weird knowing I have three mates coming out, and he might worry that he'll be on the outside. I know he won't be; the guys aren't like that and will be sensitive to it, as will I. I'm convinced he'll enjoy their company as much as I will. I hope so.

Day 8: Estella to Los Arcos

I keep receiving emails notifying me of further sponsorship. I'm blown away and I've just smashed through my new target of £3,000. This has given me such a spring in my step this morning. I was worried that the fundraising would be added stress, but I'm learning it is really helping me, and I also get some lovely messages as the donations come in, which boosts me. I'm so glad I decided to raise money for Look Sussex; this amount of money will make such a difference.

I spent an hour or so walking alone this morning, lost in my thoughts about all the people who had sponsored me. I felt warm and loved. It was warm outside too, about 26°C. In fact it has been getting steadily hotter for a couple of days now.

We did indeed pass the fuente del vino. Well, I say 'passed'; it would have been rude not to stay and sample it. I just wondered what it would be like in England on a Saturday morning if free wine flowed out of a tap. That said, two Aussie lads walked past us about twelve thirty with a two-litre bottle of water strapped to one backpack: the contents discarded, replaced with red wine!

Sadly Neil called me to say that he, Jay and Bruce couldn't get a seat on a train out of Madrid – they were all fully booked. In the UK we just cram on board! They won't get to Logroño station (about thirty kilometres away) until 10 pm, by which time the albergue I'm in will be closed – and we'll be in bed. He explained that they are going to find a hotel room in Logroño tonight and then get a taxi to me in the morning: a sign of true friendship if ever there was one. Thanks, guys.

Gabriella, the Brazilian girl who I met walking with her mum the other side of Pamplona, joined me and Chris at dinner. The three of us had a great time, sitting in a small and beautiful square drinking sangría. We then went to visit the church on the other side of the square and we couldn't believe how much gold there was. It was everywhere. This tiny little village in the middle of nowhere and the church was spectacular. together. As we entered Chris collapsed to the floor. I thought his legs had given way given the long walk today, but soon realised he was genuflecting. It was the first time I'd been into a religious place with him, and clearly his faith means a lot to him.

As we went back to our respective accommodation Gabriella said she was in a pension, with a private room and her own bathroom. We were jealous, as our accommodation was pretty grim, particularly the bathroom arrangement. We had one bathroom between thirty people. It had three showers, four sinks and two toilets. It was also mixed and there was not a urinal. It was going to be fun in the morning!

We lay in bed that night and there were some French Canadian girls amongst us. I say 'amongst'; it was more like next to us, as the bunks were so close it was like I was sharing a double bed with the girl on the top bunk next to me. In fact, had we wanted to, we could probably have kissed each other goodnight without lifting our heads from our pillows.

I was lying in bed trying to ignore my throbbing feet and my legs, which were doing their usual involuntary spasm routine, when the girl next to me burst out laughing. In her French Canadian accent she exclaimed, 'What are we doing? It is Saturday night, it's 9 pm, the sun is still up and we're in bed. We're the grown-ups, yet there are children outside playing in the street, keeping us awake.' It was a very funny moment, but so true.

Day 9: with the boys to Viana

There's something monastic about mornings in an albergue. People wake, creep out of bed, potter about, unzip and zip up zips, clip buckles and pull straps. They do their ablutions, pack, unpack and repack, rustle and finally click clips together ... but nobody speaks. It's like an unwritten rule. You might hear the faint whisper of a 'buenos días', but everyone just gets on with it, silently. I quite like it.

Also, I'm in more of a routine now. I know what goes where in my backpack, so I don't panic about leaving anything behind. I still have the peg from Orisson with me, too, which is being used most days.

We left the albergue after the usual plain bread breakfast to find the guys. They'd sent me a message to say they'd arrived and were in a café in the square. It was a great reunion and so good to see them. I introduced them to Chris and we set off for the day.

We walked 20.2 kilometres and it felt like a breeze, half fuelled by adrenaline and the other half by conversation. By 1 pm we were in Viana, which incidentally was the town where I had originally planned to meet Neil and the boys, so I wasn't too far out!

It was almost as though we weren't on a walk, as I've done nothing but laugh all day. Chris and the guys have clicked, so it's been a dream day, and the weather has been hot and sunny too. We even had time to watch the end of the Premier League season on my phone this afternoon.

Lisa video-called me from the Brooksteed. Today was the day she'd prepared tapas for the punters in support of my fundraising. It was great to see her and so many familiar faces; I feel so lucky to have the support of everyone back home. The fundraising at the pub went well, too. The tapas went down a storm and Lisa sent me a photo this morning of the chorizo, which bizarrely comes from Pamplona, where I was only three days ago!

Stu was also at the pub, so we swapped stories and I gave him tips about his training regimen. In simple terms I said, 'No matter how hard you train, it won't be enough!' At least he's training, though. I've seen some people here who don't look like they've walked to the shops and back and wonder why they're struggling, but to be fair to them, despite this, they soldier on. They might take many more weeks, if not months, to do it, but they plod on and hobble along, some of them in denim and trainers!

Unfortunately I lost my sunglasses somewhere on the trail this morning, which was disappointing.

Mass had just ended as we walked into Viana, a very old and small town celebrating its 800th year. Given it was Sunday the little streets were filled with a throng of local people. They were all following one guy who was rhythmically banging a drum to lead the way. It was quite a colourful and noisy spectacle and we couldn't have timed our arrival any better. It was as though they were waiting for us! We'd walked through barren countryside for hours with nothing but the sound of birds and our own banter, and arriving to such a throng of people and activity was a little surreal, but lovely.

We sat in the square eating some lunch opposite the church where the mass exodus (like what I did there?) was occurring. A pilgrim walked past amid the crowd, and we all offered a 'buen Camino'. As she dutifully replied I noticed she was not only wearing sunglasses but had another pair hung over the collar of her T-shirt. I thought that the chance of anyone wanting to carry the extra weight of two pairs of sunglasses was remote, so I decided to approach her. Lo and behold, they were mine. She was Spanish and seemed as pleased to reunite them with their rightful owner as I was to receive them. Make of that what you will. #TSGO!

Neil had booked a private apartment with twin rooms, so, whilst I had my best mates with me, I could still share a room with Chris. It was our Camino, after all.

We all showered and whilst we were chilling out in the lounge area my phone rang. It was Gabriella. I answered enthusiastically, but even before she spoke I could tell from her breathing that something was wrong. She was in distress.

She told me she had been walking alone through some countryside when a naked man came after her, wearing a balaclava and masturbating. She was understandably very frightened and from the way she was panting I could tell it had only just happened and she was still running away. Through sharing locations on our phones we soon established that she was about six kilometres east of Viana.

The boys were great and we kicked into gear like a slick military unit. They tried to get a taxi, but the earliest one we could get was in ninety minutes – siesta time! Neil decided to set off and started jogging back the way we'd walked earlier, in her general direction.

I spoke to some locals outside to see if they could help me get a taxi, but my limited Spanish wasn't helping. I kept making contact with Gabriella to reassure her and see that she was still OK. I then had an idea and handed my phone to a local Spanish lady whom I'd accosted in the park. Gabriella spoke Spanish. It helped. The lady was very calming and reassuring and spoke to her for a while. When they hung up she called the police. That's the Spanish police. Who turned up two hours later!

I could see from the geolocation on my phone that Neil was getting close to Gabriella, so I called them both to explain that they would soon likely bump into each other. I first called Gabriella to give her a description of Neil; the last thing she needed was to see another lone, strange man walking towards her. When I called Neil I could hear him talking reassuringly to someone. 'I've got her,' he said. Phew.

She walked back with Neil, and she was still shaking when she arrived and gave me a hug. We did the traditional British thing and made her a cup of tea. Soon she started to laugh and joke with us again, and it was good to see her get her smile back.

Neil then taunted us. He said we have a house full of fit, young, fresh-legged men, but we'd sent the oldest, the one with Parkinson's who had only just finished walking the Camino from Porto, to run up the road to rescue Gabriella. The reality is that he just went of his own volition, but it was funny, looking back on it. We'd split up to try to cover all bases and we hadn't really thought about it; instinct had taken over.

Gabriella stayed with us a few hours and once she felt ready we put her in a taxi to Logroño, some six miles west of us, where her accommodation was for tonight. We then went out for dinner and we even found a vegetarian platter in one restaurant, so Jay was really happy.

A leisurely stroll around this picturesque town followed, and, given the town's altitude compared to the surrounding landscape, we were afforded brilliant views over the plateau. We looked out to the west. Not only did Viana become host to spectacular sunsets; we could make out our path for tomorrow almost to the horizon.

Jay, me, Bruce, Neil and Chris: evening stroll around Viana

It was an eventful day. Clearly the world is full of evil people who try to take advantage, even on the Camino, maybe especially because of the Camino. Lisa has always told me it would be the ideal place to prey on vulnerable young women. The events had left a bitter taste in the mouth and I know Chris was really angry about the whole thing. The important thing is that Gabriella is safe and probably wiser because of it.

Despite those events I lay on my mattress on the floor reflecting on the good parts of the day, and there were lots of them. I'm really looking forward to another day on the path with the guys tomorrow.

I spoke with Lisa tonight. Apparently the new fridge has arrived and it is too big to get in the kitchen! I can't really do much from here, but I tried to help as best I could, suggesting she ask our neighbour for help.

Day 10: Viana to Navarrete

It started out windy and cold until about eleven and then it got hot, and hotter. Walked about twenty-two kilometres and we entered the Rioja region. We then passed through Logroño, where we popped into the massive church, and then on to our final stay in Navarrete.

Gabriella called me to arrange for us to meet her in Logroño for coffee and cake. She wanted to thank us for our help yesterday and paid for it; she said her dad had insisted. She also explained that she had met people who had unfortunately experienced a similar situation to the one yesterday, and the 'word on the path' is that the offender is a local taxi driver.

We said our goodbyes and left the sprawling conurbation of Logroño; I didn't really like it.

As we were walking through a large, beautiful park in the suburbs we came across a big guy walking the wrong way. He looked military, but he also looked disturbed by something. Some people do walk the Camino backwards, but not many do that, so, wanting to break the ice and check he was OK, Jay offered a 'buen Camino'.

His response startled us. In a broad cockney accent he shouted, 'Yeah, right, buen fucking Camino,' and in the tirade that followed, it transpired that he had been robbed and was making his way back home. He marched off at a pace, muttering to himself. We agreed that he was probably more angry with himself than anything else. It had certainly been an eventful twenty-four-hour period.

About an hour later we came to a huge lake and stopped for a break at a café. For some reason we then did some weird dad dancing to 'I Like to Move It' by Reel 2 Reel. Why? Well, it's a long story, but in simple terms Jay has been likened (by me, to be fair) to King Julien, the cartoon lemur from *Penguins of Madagascar*, and since then this has been *his* song. I danced like I'd not been walking for the last ten days. Chris just sipped coffee and looked at us like we'd all gone completely mad. He was probably right.

Neil had asked me to leave sorting the accommodation to him tonight, and he didn't disappoint. We walked through the ancient cobbled streets of Navarrete to what looked like a very old but otherwise ordinary house. He then opened the front door and there was a stonework floor like something from a Roman palace. Our jaws dropped, followed by a synchronised, choral sound of 'wow' . . . and it just got better from there.

It was the house where St Ignatius of Loyola lived, a Catholic priest who founded the Jesuit order in the sixteenth century. So, whilst it was old, it was once a palace, and the outer wall of the building was once part of the town's ramparts.

Neil even arranged for the owner, a lovely host called Georgia, to give us a private tour, not just of the house but down and down again into the wine cellars. It was incredible; the cellars were interconnected with ancient stone chutes for the wine to flow along.

Better still, the bedrooms are pretty decent too. In fact, they are so plush that, even though Chris and I have to share a double bed, we're ecstatic about it. The Camino has taught me that I really only have three main needs every day: walking, finding something to eat and somewhere to sleep. If I happen to get a shower, or, even better, an opportunity to wash my clothes, then that's a bonus. So when we walked into the room and found a large bed with white sheets, a clean, fluffy white towel, and a bedside table to put our things on, we just turned and smiled at each other: *this'll do nicely*. It is so much better than a top bunk in a packed albergue!

Of course, given that this palace has that incredible wine cellar we felt obliged to partake in some local grape juice. We then went out to find some food, and found a place in the little town square that actually advertised a vegetarian menu. It's not easy finding food for a vegetarian like Jay. It's a source of constant banter for us as he doesn't like vegetables and can't eat fish, dairy products or eggs, but we got him sorted tonight.

When we returned, Georgia explained how she was going to open up a restaurant and introduced us to her new chef. Apparently they will open it next month. I simply have to come back here with Lisa. It's an amazing place and she'd love it. The wine's not bad either!

I called Lisa. She had invited Cara and our friends Steffie and Peter round to watch *The Way*, as they hadn't seen the film. It was humbling to think that they were there doing that, to get a taste of what I was going through right now.

Day 11: Navarrete to Azofra

It's been awesome having the guys come out and see me and I know Chris has really appreciated their company too. He told me last night that he was going to miss them. Sadly they will leave us at the end of today.

After we'd been walking for an hour I received some lovely texts from Cara all about the film. Apparently she had walked the Camino in her dreams last night. If only it was that easy.

My brother Richard also called me this morning. He said he'd woken up, looked at the app I was using and noticed I'd already been walking for forty minutes, so he'd decided to call me. It was fabulous to hear from him whilst on the trail and we had a good laugh, as we always do when we speak.

Just after I spoke with him, we came to a long gentle climb of about four kilometres, which unfortunately ran parallel to a main highway. We hadn't been near any busy roads for days, so I was initially disappointed. However, to my surprise the motorists were great, as every now and then a passing lorry driver or car owner would toot their horn and wave us on our way. It was really quite special to think that they knew what we were doing and it helped to break the monotony of the climb as we kept raising our hands to wave back with gratitude.

Shortly afterwards I bumped into Bakjé from Rotterdam, who was either an inspiration or seriously lost. Let me explain. Our conversation went something like this:

Me: Hola. Buenos días.
Her: Buen Camino.
Me: Gracias; do you speak English?
Her: Yes. I am from Rotterdam.
Me: Where did you start your Camino? In St Jean?
Her: I am from Rotterdam.
Me: *(thinking it was a language thing)* Yes, I understood that, but where did you start the Camino?
Her: In Rotterdam!

She was walking alone, said goodbye to her husband and children back in Holland on 23 February. She'd already walked 2,500 kilometres. I thought I had a long walk ahead of me! I kept thinking of her all afternoon as each footstep got more painful and thought to myself, *Stop complaining; you could still be walking through the middle of France to get to the start!*

I mentioned her to Stu on the phone. He said she probably just put her coat on and shouted to her husband, 'I'm just popping to the shops to get some milk,' and he's still sitting there waiting for his cuppa!

I was so glad we had the boys with us again today, which really helped to create some laughs. Chris, Neil and I were about a kilometre from our lunch stop and my feet were killing me. We couldn't see Bruce or Jay as they'd walked slightly faster, then suddenly Bruce jumped up out of some concrete tubing, followed by Jay doing a Lion King impression on top of what looked just like Pride Rock with his shirt off; it was hilarious.

Today was hard going, though. The terrain wasn't too challenging, but the heat, distance and I guess general wear and tear are taking their toll.

Chris and I checked into a decent hostel and said a very sad goodbye to the boys. We both agreed our feet felt really tired. It wasn't helped by the fact that for the last 4.5 kilometres it was about 26°C and there was one tree for the whole stretch, which we all sat under, just happy to get some shade.

I've just spent the last hour tending to blisters on my feet; they have finally decided to make an appearance. Time to try out the top tips I got from Jason Fox, I thought. Without going into details, they involve a needle, thread and zinc oxide tape.

Chris also has a blister, but bizarrely it is on his hand, where the skin has rubbed against his walking poles. It looks pretty sore, actually, but at least he doesn't have to put his body weight on it, unlike mine. Yes, I'm feeling a bit sorry for myself. Probably a combination of pain, fatigue and having just said goodbye to the boys.

I spoke with Lisa after I had a shower and she said, 'You sound tired.' I was.

Chris and I did some washing and headed out for our pilgrim dinner – another three courses with wine for € 10. We hardly spoke to each other over dinner; we were shattered. Early start tomorrow and another twenty-five kilometres too, and just the two of us again.

Day 12: Azofra to Redecilla

We left early today, as planned to beat the heat. My blisters hurt within the first few steps, but there was no choice, I decided, so I tried to ignore the pain and after about 500 metres it seemed to work.

At ten thirty we sang along to our daily tunes and then I fancied something upbeat, so I chose Tina Turner's live version of 'Proud Mary'. Chris asked me what made me want to play it and I told him it just came to me as a fairly upbeat song to walk along to. He explained that it was Karen's favourite song, and that it was played at her funeral. There really is something going on.

We walked past a big industrial/storage unit and the smell immediately took me back to working on my grandparents' fruit and veg market stall in Dudley during my school holidays. It was a massive potato warehouse with spuds in crates as far as the eye could see. It was so reminiscent of the earthy smell I was accustomed to up that end of the stall. 'Panj pound chaalees pennies' (five pounds for 40p, if I've recalled that correctly) to the local Indian community back then – happy memories indeed.

I walked on thinking about the good times I'd had on the stall with my grandparents, aunts, uncles and cousins. It was the central magnet for our family and helped to shape my personality in many ways.

It then dawned on me after a while how long I'd spent thinking about all of this from just a scent. We're talented creatures when we have the time and freedom to let our brains wander. I'm enjoying doing that right now. It's liberating out here.

We had a very comical lunch in Santo Domingo. We sat outside a café on a small cobbled street, enjoying a view of the cathedral and eating sandwiches. There was a fiesta going on and it was apparently due to come down the street we were in. As a consequence, the waiters were poised, ready to pounce and take away chairs and tables as quickly as they could; it was due any minute. We didn't dare stand up! As soon as anyone did his or her chair was whisked away, as happened to a Mexican pilgrim behind me, much to the amusement of everyone sitting around. The staff rushed us to eat our food as quickly as we could.

Then the mood suddenly changed. We all worked out that the fiesta had obviously made a detour and was no longer coming down this little street as the waiters began huffing and puffing and putting the tables and chairs back out. It was like a silent comedy that crossed all language barriers, evident from the hysterical laughter from all nationalities of pilgrims who had witnessed the whole event. The waiters weren't so happy. As it happened the fiesta was something and nothing, but the traditional costumes worn by all the children were quite impressive.

Gemma, the girl in my team at work who gave me my journal at Christmas, is due to get married in a week's time. I thought it would be a nice touch to send her a Spanish wedding card direct from the Camino, so I made Chris traipse around the town as we tried to find a card shop that was open. Sadly, once we'd found a shop and bought a card, the post offices were closed, so that would have to wait until we got to another big town.

After lunch we crossed the Rio Oja and, by doing so, left Rioja country and entered our next region, Castile and León. Almost instantly the vineyards seemed to stop, replaced by crops of wheat and potato fields. It explained the large potato factory we walked past earlier.

At the top of the next hill I received a video call from Mum. Once I'd explained to her that I was indeed taking on enough fluids and that there were plenty of places to get water, she seemed OK; I guess you never stop fussing as a parent! She also insisted on seeing my blisters, which gave me a good excuse to change my socks, a practice I've introduced when it is hot. I recycle them by hanging the worn pair on my backpack so I always have a nice dry pair to put on; well, I say 'nice'! Actually, it was great to hear from Mum and she sent me a lovely text afterwards. Knowing how long it takes her to type, it meant a lot. It was quite long and was really beautiful.

65

We stopped in a village about 3 pm and had a little clara con limon. This is the Spanish equivalent of a British shandy, beer with a lemon mixer; it's quite refreshing on a hot day. Laurel recommended clara to us back in Pamplona. It was 25°C without any breeze and our drinks slipped down easily, so we ordered another.

We considered ditching the last five kilometres but forced ourselves to plough on. It was a slog, though. I listened to an audiobook, as I tend to do for the end-of-day kilometres; they are always longer, much longer. Just when I needed a boost Jimbo called me, and before I knew it we were on the outskirts of our destination.

And I thought that was enough fun for one day. But oh, how wrong I was. The man who runs the albergue I'm staying in tonight is as mad as a box of frogs. He is like Basil Fawlty crossed with David Icke. When we checked in we unfortunately decided to pay for a pilgrim meal at the albergue before we realised our host was two sandwiches short of a picnic.

Our host told us we were sharing a room with a German couple, but they had gone out for dinner. Perhaps they had twigged and decided to eat elsewhere. At least the showers were clean and the bunks seem OK.

Chris then noticed there was a reflexologist across the road, so we went to explore. She was great. She walked the Camino in 1999 and decided to set up in this desolate village to help pilgrims. There was no set price either as she only accepted donations. If your feet are hurting and you can't afford to pay, then that's acceptable; she'll still treat you. I put a generous donation in the box in the wall on the way out. Needless to say, between us, Chris and I probably made her day; she certainly made mine.

With renewed and revitalised feet, a waft of lavender oils and an air of trepidation we made our way to dinner.

Our host, whom Chris quickly nicknamed 'the Crazy Juan', was entertaining, to say the least! You could send psychology students here for weeks and they themselves would go crazy trying to work him out. Chris and I cried laughing at our intimate dinner for four, which consisted of us two, a really nice French chap and Basil Icke himself. There was no sign of the German couple. Crazy Juan kept making funny farting noises with his mouth and at one time walked in with an apple pie, pretending to trip and turning the dish upside down for effect. Apparently he does it every night. When he explained that he cooked the same meal every night, and had done so for the last three years, we all nearly lost the plot. Our sides hurt so much, and he just laughed along with us. Don't get me wrong, soup, pasta and apple pie is nice, but every day for over 1,000 days on the trot?

I left and called Rich. I just had to share it with someone.

We bumped into the German couple. They thought the owner was 'kranken', so they'd chosen to eat in the square. They'd missed a real treat!

Day 13: Redecilla to Villafranca

We woke to find Herr German standing stark bollock naked on the balcony, displaying all and sundry to passing pilgrims. Thankfully I just got the saggy view from behind. Chris and I quietly, gently eased our way to the bathroom and hoped he'd be dressed by the time we returned; thankfully he was. His name was Wolf, he said he was a musician on German TV, and he was a lovely character.

Like football, today would be a game of two halves. After breakfast Wolf started playing the guitar, accompanied by Crazy Juan on the harmonica. We had a good singalong too, and it was a fun and lively start to the day.

Then we started walking and my feet really hurt. It was a tough, long day. I couldn't be bothered to get my phone out to take any photos, and to be honest the countryside wasn't brilliant as we were alongside the main road for most of the day.

I bumped into Angela, a lady we met outside the church in Azofra three nights ago. She seemed delighted to see us and explained that today was her last day on the Camino. She said she wanted to talk with me and had been praying that she would bump into me today. In her opinion, the fact that she succeeded meant that the Lord had provided. I'm not sure why she wanted to talk to me; other than a brief exchange in the square I hardly knew her. In fact, the only thing I knew about her was that she was from Liverpool.

Anyway, she was very pleasant and we walked and talked. After a while I felt comfortable enough to tell her that when we met her the other night my friend Neil thought she was a nun. At that point she simply burst into tears and collapsed on the track. Uh-oh!

She said, 'You have no idea how much that means to me.'

I was pleased to discover that I probably couldn't have said anything better to her. I'm glad I did. It really made her day, that's for sure. She joined us for a coffee and we said our goodbyes as Chris and I had much further to walk today.

I'm amazed at how much wheat is grown in northern Spain. Today was endless rolling hills of the stuff, from horizon to horizon.

I asked Chris if he'd heard about the myth that, when the wind blows the wheat and it sways in unison, it is the spirits of the dead whispering back to us. He'd not heard this, and about twenty minutes later, as we crested the top of a hill, to our right was the most enormous wheat field where the wind was working its magic. The wheat was swaying in one direction, towards us, then swirling round and down to a corner in the field, as though it was pointing the way along the path. It was quite a marvellous spectacle; I'd never seen anything like it on such a grand scale. I hesitated before plucking up the courage to say, 'Look, there you go, Chris. Karen's whispering to us, showing us the way to go.'

I carried on walking, admiring the spectacle. When I got to the corner I turned around to talk to Chris, but he wasn't there. I looked back up the path to find him standing dead still on the crest of that hill, having not moved from where we'd last spoken. He was lost in thought, just staring at the wheat. I left him to it. I was glad I'd told him. He'll no doubt catch me later. #TSGO!

The albergue that we are staying in is a pretty, peaceful place, but when I got into the shower the water kept stopping every few minutes. I got really fed up and had a bit of a low point. I've had enough of all of this; my feet are hurting and I can't even have a hot shower. I told myself that this is what the Camino is about, but it didn't help; I've had enough.

Chris could see I was down, so he took me out for a beer. As if by magic Lisa called me at that moment and I really enjoyed talking to her. I just listened and lost myself in her day.

We found a little bar; well, actually a little bench in someone's garden, but they sold beer in cans, so we weren't complaining.

I noticed that three more people had sponsored me today. It gave me a boost, and I started to send my thank-you notes, but intriguingly I didn't recognise one of the people. Once I'd worked out how to retrieve the email address I managed to deduce that the mysterious donation was from Angela! Heaven knows how she had traced me; we only loosely talked about my fundraising, and she doesn't even know my surname!

Chris then told me that, as tomorrow would have been Karen's birthday, he's paying for a nice hotel for us both to stay in. You accept graciously when others give on the Camino, and his timing was perfect; he knew it would perk me up.

All three have lifted my mood; that's Lisa, the sponsorship and Chris, not the beer! It's supposed to rain tomorrow, so I've decided I might as well enjoy this beer in some sunshine while I can.

There was some serious snoring going on by the time we got back to our albergue, but, on the plus side, at least we weren't in bunks tonight.

Day 14: Villafranca to Burgos

I hardly got any sleep. During the night the fat woman opposite me only stopped snoring like a juggernaut to look at her mobile phone and then started again. The other fourteen people in our room didn't snore, probably due to her decibels keeping them awake too. On top of that I had an upset tummy and, oh, how I longed for my own toilet!

Pilgrims donning full waterproofs is not a quiet exercise and the rain was upon us the moment we left the albergue. It was an immediate, very steep climb, with no time to warm up the legs today. It was rocky too, and once at the top we were faced with six kilometres of wet, slippery sand. It was cold (4°C) and very windy, yet despite all of this, and in stark contrast to yesterday's mood, I loved it. I felt fit, I had waterproofs and I just thought to myself, *You've carried them for two weeks; now's the chance to use them.* I embraced it. I was dry and warm and getting exercise in the fresh air. What more could I ask for?

Trying to ignore the pain from the blisters, we set a good pace. Chris and I walked solidly for three hours without stopping or really talking to each other. We hardly saw anyone else either. Sometimes he'd be 200 metres in front and then we'd end up swapping places, as we changed into or out of our waterproofs, or took a quick photo in the rain, with just a cursory nod, wink or 'all good?' as we passed to check in on each other.

I was really enjoying the solitude, the sound of the rain on my waterproof hood, and the rhythmic crunch of my footsteps on the sandy path. My feet were enjoying the softer, wetter sand too. Whilst the wet sand made it hard going, my blisters were happier. My mind wandered; I loved it.

69

We'd walked twelve kilometres by 9.30 am. I was starving but I was even enjoying the hunger. That said, when we stumbled into the next village at 10.15 am the empanadas didn't touch the sides!

I also received a call from Martyn, just as the rain stopped, and it was good to chat with him. As he put it, 'I'm just checking in on my favourite munchkin!' Mum also called me and we had a good laugh, recounting the stories about Crazy Juan from two nights ago.

We then walked for another six kilometres through wilderness and a diseased forest of dead oak trees, which in the low cloud and cool breeze was quite spooky. Before we got to the next village, Agés, someone had written in graffiti on a signpost, 'It takes ages to get to Agés!' – we knew how they felt.

We could see the spires of Burgos for miles and it seemed to take forever to trudge through the paved suburbs until we reached the historic city centre. El Cid is buried in the cathedral here.

We've now got 304 miles left. When I worked out that we'd walked 190 miles I chuckled, as that's the distance from my house to my mum's in the West Midlands, and I'd never walk there!

When we arrived we checked in to the hotel Chris had booked, showered and limped around the city; it's so much easier without a backpack. Burgos is really pretty. We found time to look around the magnificent cathedral.

He is treating me to dinner tonight and he keeps threatening champagne. We've got another long day tomorrow, but nowhere near as long as today, thankfully. I found a post office, too, and was delighted to get Gemma's wedding card in the post.

Dinner was fantastic. We asked the hotel receptionist where the best pulpo (octopus) in town was and we headed straight there. I've never eaten anything so delicious. And yes, Chris bought champagne and, rather touchingly, he poured a glass for Karen. We toasted her birthday. He did it in style. We ate and drank like kings. The total bill including the champagne was only €80, so the waitress got a healthy tip as she had been brilliant all night.

Now for some sleep. We're knackered, but well fed and watered. Hopefully my blisters will get better overnight with champagne in my bloodstream; that is a recognised treatment strategy, right?

Day 15: Burgos to Hornillos del Camino

Leaving the urban sprawl of Burgos was boring, but we soon experienced our first tabletop plateau: two kilometres up, two kilometres flat and two kilometres down. We have two more to do tomorrow and they make it interesting.

We nearly walked straight past a little gem of a monastery in Rabé de las Calzadas, but we heard some enchanting music that enticed us in. It was a pretty little place. For some reason the nuns made a beeline for Chris and they both gave him little gifts. I know it meant a lot to him.

I also met some old faces today that I haven't seen since week one, some from day one. This seems to happen whenever you get to a big city. There were some lovely moments when we walked past and recognised each other, followed by a warm embrace and a wish of 'buen Camino'.

Of note for me was Wes, a great young guy from Taiwan. I hadn't seen him since Pamplona, but he's now suffering with tendinitis, so he's going a bit slower. It was great to catch up on the past week or so as I walked with him to the next village, where he would stop for the day. Buen Camino, Wes.

We didn't have as much rain as forecast today, so that was a bonus. We covered twenty-one kilometres and wanted to do another five, but we discovered the accommodation in the village we were aiming for was full. So we stopped in Hornillos del Camino at 2.30 pm and relaxed.

The albergue tonight is a small, friendly place. A maximum of ten pilgrims per room, €10 a bed, hopefully with no severe snorers! Also we had a communal pilgrim meal tonight cooked by the owners, a huge chicken and chorizo paella served in one of those large woks. We were well fed, and we only paid another €7 for the meal, which included bread and wine, of course. Well, I say we paid; Chris secretly paid. He keeps doing that. I'll make sure it evens itself out over the coming weeks.

I'm now in my top bunk. I've just watched the Giro d'Italia cycling highlights on my phone and I'm getting ready to watch the FA Cup final between Man City and Watford. I need City to win so Wolves get a European place; that would be dreamland!

Claudia is in our room. In fact she's on the bunk below me. She's great, about seventy years old, from Argentina. Married, but here alone. She has a huge silver suitcase, so it's obvious she isn't carrying her stuff every day and is calling upon the Camino transport services. I've not used them, and have no intention of doing so unless I really have to.

It's just hit me that it's three weeks to the day before I will get to see Lisa in Santiago (hopefully), and only one week until Stu comes out. I'm taking each day as it comes and I'm not wishing the time away, because it's a privilege to be here, but I am missing Lisa a lot today. Still, City won, so that's lifted my mood a little.

The snoring has begun. But the good news is that Lisa told me the fridge is now in situ!

Day 16: Hornillos del Camino to Castrojeriz

It is at this point that I need to tell you about Chris's dreadful sense of direction. Sometimes I think he's only walking with me because if he was walking alone he'd be heading towards Italy by now.

Hornillos del Camino is typical of 80% of the hamlets to be found on the Camino. You see them from about five kilometres away, as the church spire comes into view. As you approach the hamlet, and the church spire gets bigger, you realise that the buildings on the way in are either in ruin or in desperate need of repair. These hamlets usually consist of just one street and if you're lucky your albergue might be one of the best-maintained buildings on the street, second only to the church. If the place is thriving, there may be a bar or restaurant offering some competition to the albergues. One thing is crystal clear: if it wasn't for the passing trade of pilgrims they would be completely desolate ghost towns.

So, after you've approached Hornillos del Camino from the east and stopped at the albergue on your right-hand side, you'd naturally expect Chris, upon leaving the albergue this morning, to turn right and head west. He didn't. At first I thought he was winding me up again with his dry sense of humour, so I let him carry on a bit and followed him. He started getting into his stride. What's he doing? The sun's up, for fuck's sake, it's in front of us; surely he knows we should be walking west!

A small group of pilgrims walked towards us, and through puzzled glances offered us a curious 'buen Camino', at which point he turned round, inquisitively, only to see my face creased up with laughter. He hasn't got a Scooby when it comes to directions. It was a great start to the day, though.

It was cold to start off, mist was in the air, but it turned out hot. I got a text from Chris Croke early this morning. I called him straight back. I'm so lucky to have a brother-in-law who's more of a best mate. We had a good chat until I lost signal, which didn't come back for about four hours! Ho-hum, at least the freedom was fabulous.

The walk was beautiful today, with so many spring colours in the fields. It was a lovely twenty-kilometre Sunday stroll and my feet also feel a bit better. I even walked the last eight kilometres in sandals, which seemed to really help my blisters.

The highlight of the day for me was being alone on a plateau. There was no one within 500 metres of me and I was listening to music, singing at the top of my voice to Coldplay. I loved it. It was so liberating. I sounded brilliant, too; watch out, Chris Martin!

Watch out, Chris Martin!

We could see our destination at Castrojeriz in the distance. It was a long straight road and created the illusion the town was nearer than it was. After forty minutes we could still see it. Someone had written on a road sign, 'Are we there yet?' and I could see why.

When we eventually arrived we were not disappointed. I thought it was beautiful, very different to the less glowing description my guidebook offered. It's a town on different levels, quaint and picturesque, with an old monastery carved into the hilltop overlooking the town.

Now that I had a phone signal, I finally caught up with Chris too.

The other Chris, the one I'm walking with, is currently a bit drunk! We've just finished eating at a local steak maestro's home. Being a Yank, Chris has been craving his meat, and we've had our protein fix tonight, that's for sure. I'm not sure he'll be able to walk back to the room tonight, though; we're about to find out!

We have a long day tomorrow (twenty-eight kilometres) and I'm feeling ready for it. I really hope my feet are. I just realised it will be Monday morning tomorrow, too; that is a lovely thought given I'm here and not going to work.

Day 17: Castrojeriz to Población de Campos

Lots happened today as we walked over twenty-eight kilometres. I say 'over' because we were so tired when we arrived in Población de Campos that we walked straight past our accommodation. It was the very first building in the village and we ended up walking around like lost souls trying to find it, unable to use our phones because for some reason the batteries had died today.

We found two pilgrims, already cleanly washed and on their way back from a local taverna. They took pity on us and pointed us in the right direction. Imagine how we felt once we realised we had to walk back to where we'd first entered the town, about another 500 metres. That might not sound far, but at the end of a long day, when all you want to do is get a shower, it is. At least the nice couple walked with us to the door so we didn't get lost again.

Despite this, it was a great day. I had the best Monday morning ever. It started with a really steep climb, but the sun was shining, we'd slept well and, having eaten very well the night before, we were full of energy. Better still, my blisters were on the mend. I kept thinking about people at work; not about work itself, but the fact that work felt so far away and I was enjoying Monday mornings again.

I contemplated how I had really switched off out here. The times when I walk alone provide some great opportunities to reflect and enter a very calm state. It's difficult to describe, but when you're walking for a couple of hours, you can see the path ahead and there's nothing around you for miles other than beautiful rolling greenscape there's not really much to do or think about. Add to that the rhythmic, almost hypnotic sound of my own footsteps, the constant birdsong, a slight breeze, warmth on my skin, and my backpack feeling ever more like it's just a part of me, and it all adds up to a really happy place: one where you enter a meditative state as the brain becomes empty. It happens rarely in my world, but being able to condition the brain so that it stops thinking about anything in particular is something I'm learning and getting better at. It is uplifting.

And then it happened. As I walked I had a strange feeling, which had happened to me before, but I'd dismissed it. I kept turning around or moving to one side of the path to let other pilgrims pass, but every time I did there was nobody there. I thought nothing of it at first, but it kept happening, and it was always on my left side. It was weird. It was like there was someone walking with me. Maybe, just maybe, there was.

I was convinced there was someone walking next to me

The weather was much warmer today, and around 2 pm it turned incredibly toasty! We walked for seven hours with lots of breaks to rest our feet.

I met three girls from China, South Korea and Malaysia this afternoon. They had all initially been travelling alone, but they had met out here and were now friends. One writes as a journalist for a Catholic magazine in China; I think my photo might be appearing in the next edition!

As the heat of the day began to rise we were pleasantly surprised to discover that the Camino joined a canal path at Juan de Homar. We also came across a jetty offering boat trips, 'St James' Way on a Boat', which would take us to the next village, some five kilometres away along the water, with a reduced price for pilgrims of €2. What a fabulous idea, we thought, and then we realised we'd missed the one boat for today. Still, the canal made for a change of scenery, plus where there's water there's usually vegetation, and here it was in the form of trees. They offered some welcome shade from the roasting sun.

I have to be honest, though: the last 3.8 kilometres into our town tonight were a slog, particularly as they were dead straight alongside a quiet road. And this was before we got lost.

The shower was definitely needed and I stood in it with my clothes on to wash them too, partly because it was practical, but primarily because I didn't have the energy to take them off. The good news, I told Chris, is that I think we cross the halfway point tomorrow.

The albergue host was wonderful. She cooked us a fabulous peregrino (pilgrim) meal. She even did all her hair and make-up for dinner, and came out of the kitchen to greet us afterwards and check if everything was OK. It was like having your grandmother come round to cook for you and your friends. You can often feel the pride people take from being able to serve pilgrims, and our host tonight treated us as though it was a privilege for *her*. There are some beautiful people in this world. We ate with a couple of German guys, a girl from Switzerland and a chap from Argentina. After today's work, it was fuel my body badly needed.

I'm trying to get some sleep. My feet are pounding, though, and they feel like I'm still walking on them.

Day 18: Población de Campos to Carrión de los Condes

Chris and I decided to choose a longer route today in order to miss walking alongside the main road. I'm so glad we did. The frog chorus and birdsong along the riverbank was like something from a BBC nature documentary. We walked in silence just listening to it.

I found myself thinking about all the wonderful people I'd met on my journey so far, probably triggered by the lovely lady who served us dinner last night: people like Natalia, the host of the albergue in Puente la Reina. These are really special people. We were treated as though we were the only guests they'd welcomed for months, but the reality is they get new guests every day, and they're unlikely to ever see them again. They don't exactly need to win your business back, but there's a genuine kindness, compassion, a sense of understanding, and they really have left their mark on me. They take such pride in helping.

It was at that moment I decided I would take a leaf out of their book. When I return home, I am going to find a way to fit some volunteering or charity work into my schedule.

I started to explore options. I'd love to work with kids, but then I think I'd find myself getting too upset and wanting to bring them home. The more I thought about it, the more I realised that opportunities were endless, but the important thing is that I am going to do something. The Camino has spoken to me. #TSGO!

I received calls from both Mike and James, just checking in on how their old man was doing.

Lunch was in a fabulous little town called Villalcázar. We sat in a square offering one area of shade, and underneath sat pilgrims, many of whom we recognised. It was lively. It was also opposite a church, which had a huge doorway through which you unusually entered from the south. There was a funeral underway, and all the pilgrims were waiting for it to finish so that they could then have a look inside the church. This meant more time to drink red wine in the sun, which added to the atmosphere!

It was only 1.30 pm, so it was far too early for us to join them. They had finished walking for the day, but Chris and I intended to walk further.

We also feel more accustomed to walking in the heat. I say 'we'; I mean me. Chris is from Trinidad, so he's used to it. I wear a full-brimmed sunhat and paint myself in factor 50 every day; he doesn't even apply sun cream, and I've only seen him put a hat on a couple of times.

Oh, and in my complete tiredness last night I miscalculated the halfway point. Chris and I worked out I was a day out! We were quite disappointed, but it gives us something to look forward to tomorrow.

We're staying in a large convent, so it felt appropriate to go to six o'clock

Another factor 50 day.

mass tonight, and at the end there was a special pilgrim blessing for all pilgrims in town. It was really quite tastefully done.

Afterwards we ate a pilgrim meal in the square opposite a huge block of granite. It had 'Santiago 401km' etched into the side, along with an arrow pointing the way out of town. At least we knew where we'd be heading in the morning!

We ate with Werner, a lovely German chap, sixty-five years young, who was now on his way back from Santiago on his bike, cycling to Düsseldorf. Whilst he had an e-bike, that is still a pretty impressive achievement. Further still, he said that he was thinking of swinging by Carcassonne in the south of France to see his son who is based there; hats off to Werner.

The combination of good food, company and mingling with locals in the square tonight created a pleasant evening, but one where we also lost track of the time. We had to rush back to the albergue and we just beat the nine-thirty curfew. The nuns had already turned all the lights off and all eleven of the other people in our room were tucked up in bed. Some were on their phones, but the snoring had already commenced from others – great.

The main snorer is a very elderly Spanish chap who speaks no English, and I tried to have a brief conversation with him earlier before dinner. He spoke so quickly I failed. He was also tired and I think wanted to get to bed early anyway. I guess he who falls asleep first doesn't have to put up with the snoring of others; maybe that was his strategy. Boring, though, and we'd had a great night in the square whilst he slept.

We have eighteen kilometres of nothing ahead of us tomorrow: no shade, no water, no cafés, nothing but what the Spanish call 'la meseta' (the plateau). Sounds fun!

I've got to go; Sister Margaret Mary (or whatever her name is) has just been in with her torch to make sure we're all tucked up!

Day 19: Carrión de los Condes to Ledigos

Our guidebook described the meseta as eighteen kilometres of 'a featureless plain', and I can't think of a better description. I took very few photos; there was nothing to capture, other than the path itself, which was just dead straight and flat. The only thing to look at was my shadow, which, because we were walking west, was always in front of me, decreasing in size as the sun rose overhead.

Always time to take a good look at yourself

There was a pop-up caravan offering coffee from a flask after about ten kilometres, which was a pleasant surprise, but that was the highlight of our morning.

It was as challenging mentally as it was physically, a day for music, audiobooks, podcasts and singing – anything to break the monotony. There was lots of thinking time, too. Oh, and my invisible friend kept making its presence felt – weird. On top of all this, it was roasting hot; there were very few clouds in the sky, and no shade whatsoever. When we eventually arrived at a little village (Calzadilla de la Cueza) for lunch, it really felt like an oasis in the desert.

There was an albergue in the village with a swimming pool. It looked inviting. We bumped into the pilgrim from Switzerland who we'd eaten with two nights ago. She was staying there, and she said the last thing she'd do was get in that pool. 'Just imagine how many grimy pilgrims have been in there for a bath,' she added. She probably had a point.

Chris went inside the café to use the toilet and when he returned he had a weird swagger about him. When he sat down, he pulled out a huge blade (a 'piece', as he called it) and placed it on the table. He did this without losing eye contact with the owner. I wondered what on earth had happened. Apparently he thought the owner was giving him 'the eye' and was being confrontational. I just laughed and told him to chill out. This is Europe, not America.

We rested for about an hour and a half and then ploughed on for the final 6.4 kilometres. We were convinced we'd walked further as it seemed to take forever.

With about two kilometres to go, I started to get delirious. I wasn't sure whether it was something I'd eaten at lunch or I was getting sunstroke: a real possibility as the temperature was well into the mid-thirties, although I'd already drunk over three litres of water. I was concerned, and because I was feeling dizzy I asked Chris to keep an eye on me. Bless him; he walked very closely behind me all the way into the village.

We saw no one else for the final hour and a half, probably because it was so hot. For the last 500 metres I was sucking on my water bladder with everything I'd got, trying to get every last drop out.

I started to feel a little better for having had a shower and resting in some shade. I thought the old snoring Spanish bloke in our albergue last night was crazy when he got up at three o'clock this morning to walk in the dark; maybe he knew how hot it was going to be. Us white English office boys just aren't used to it!

There would be none of those disturbances tonight, though. Chris and I are in an albergue, but we have a private room with our own bathroom. We ate out under a canopied terrace, more seafood and a tiny bit of vino, given I was drinking water by the gallon.

We finally passed the halfway point too: 380 kilometres left, or 236 miles. A few days ago Stu sent me a track to listen to as we crossed it. It's called 'Breathe In' by Daddy Was a Milkman and the words are so appropriate. It really is a wonderful song, and I think it will end up becoming my song of the year. It's already now part of our daily Camino playlist along with 'He Ain't Heavy, He's My Brother' by the Hollies.

Anyway, despite the sunstroke symptoms today, the legs felt good and my blisters are nowhere near as painful as they were a few days ago. Thank the Lord for Compeed!

Day 20: Ledigos to Sahagún

During breakfast Claudia, the Argentinian lady with the large silver suitcase, came by and complained about her leg. Chris had worked as a personal trainer for a US gym chain, so without hesitation he was up. Within a few seconds he had her performing some yoga-type pose, her foot up behind her back whilst he supported her, head leaning down to the floor. Not your usual sight over breakfast, but she seemed very grateful.

Today was, without the shadow of a doubt, my best day on the Camino. I felt that I reached a deep state of relaxation. It normally takes me a while to switch off from work when I have a holiday, and it did when I took my sabbatical at the beginning of May, but today normal life seemed a million miles away. It felt great. I don't particularly know why. It was maybe a combination of factors; having our own room last night was blissful, and the good food and ten hours' solid sleep will also have helped. I'm now into my fourth week away from work, and that was probably the biggest contributor.

The weather was much kinder to us too, with more cloud, less heat and a cooler breeze. I wore my sandals all day, and my feet enjoyed the change of footwear and being in the air.

Walking in sandals made a refreshing change

We were coming across villages faster than we expected. We found a great little café for a spot of lunch, and then Chris came out with the quote of the day: 'It is so beautiful out here. In fact, the whole thing would be so lovely if it wasn't for the goddamn walking.'

Having read my comments on the app I'm using, Søs from Denmark sent me a message regarding yesterday's challenges. It went along the lines of 'If you expect it to be plain and boring, Simon, it will be. Instead, look for the magic in every day.' I guess, in retrospect, she was right. She was telling me off in a polite way, but it made me think about how I had approached yesterday, and how maybe, with a different attitude, it could have been a different experience. Just like any other day, really. The attitude you adopt when you get out of bed can often affect how your day pans out. The Camino had yet again given me a little lesson about everyday life; it does that to you.

Today has definitely been magic. Just before we got to Sahagún, we crossed another halfway point, but this time it was for the Spanish. They don't start in France and cross the Pyrenees like most other nationalities, but start in Roncesvalles (day three for me). It was very pretty and peaceful and the point was marked by a pretty stone gateway. Chris and I lay there under the trees, soaking it in and enjoying the shade and silence. We were the only ones around for a long period and I fell asleep on a marble bench, looking up at the trees and blue sky beyond.

When I came to, I said to Chris, 'This is just brilliant; I'd never get the opportunity to just sit and waste an hour on a Wednesday afternoon like this,' to which he just laughed and replied, 'It's Thursday!' I don't wear a watch out here; I never know what the time is, as all I really need to know is sunrise and sunset, but now I've forgotten what day it is too.

What I do know, though, is that Lisa is in Barcelona with some school friends today for a well-deserved mini-break. There's something really comforting about knowing that she's now in the same country as me. We're still miles apart – she's on the east coast and I'm walking west – but she seems closer, and that makes me feel good.

The tastefully done 'Spanish halfway' monument

Sahagún is a large town and quite lively. It's very different to our stop last night, where the total population was only about thirty and the pilgrims outnumbered the locals by three to one!

We had a great evening, as we were joined by lots of pilgrims and we just sat chatting and laughing. They were from Texas, Hawaii, Brazil, Florida, California and Canada. There was also a South African lady who lived, of all places, in Fourth Avenue, Hove, not too far from my home.

Day 21: Sahagún to Reliegos

We woke to blue skies but we were slightly taken aback as we stepped outside; the wind chill was biting. We took a slightly different route to avoid following the road. It was the route that Emperor Augustus had used, so we thought if it was good enough for him ...

It was a mistake. The surface was so uneven that after about three hours we were in agony. Our knees and calves were aching from the rocking and twisting. A quick look at Google Maps showed us that there might be a track back to the original Camino, but it meant crossing the mainline railway from León to Madrid and we weren't sure whether we could. Thankfully, two kilometres later, we were back on the looser gravel of the normal Camino.

At that point Lisa video-called me, laughing ironically because it was pouring down in Barcelona and she could see blue sky all around me here. Still, it sounded like she was having a great time.

There's been a sickness bug doing the rounds and it has been the main topic on the Camino grapevine for a few days. Four nights ago there was a girl in our albergue who was throwing up and there have been more stories of victims. We're hoping to avoid it. Chris blames salad-eaters; he said, 'That's why I eat meat. Salad is where you get germs from.' Whilst we laughed about it, I knew he was dead serious!

As we walked further along the normal Camino route it began to look familiar and I soon realised it was the section of the route I'd walked two years earlier. We approached Reliegos (yes, that's really the name of the town), where last time I'd stayed in what I can only describe as a shitty albergue. We were hungry, so we went straight into the first albergue we saw and ordered some lunch. Given the food was excellent and the host was really welcoming, I chanced asking if they had any private rooms. Bingo – a massive triple room for the two of us.

I took Chris into the town to show him the other albergues. He's so glad we booked in at the first one. We also visited Bar Elvis, a famous bar on the Camino as it featured in the film *The Way*.

Today marks the end of week three. I'm excited about Stu joining us in León tomorrow night. I'm sure he'll love it out here – apart from the walking, that is!

Day 22: Reliegos to León

We got our first proper glimpse of the big mountains on the horizon beyond León today. They will soon be upon us, in three to four days' time.

León used to be Spain's capital city and is therefore pretty huge. There's an unusual custom in León: tapas comes free with every drink. So we went into the city having already decided we were very, very hungry!

We had a chilled afternoon in the city, strolling around (yes, more walking) from bar to cathedral to basilica to café and back to bar. I did, however, remember to buy Lisa an anniversary card, figuring this might be the last opportunity for me to get one before Santiago, and I'd rather be safe than sorry.

We'd intended on meeting Stu tonight, but we were tired, so we went on the bus back to our hotel, which was just on the outskirts of the city, for an earlier night. We have twenty-six kilometres tomorrow, so it'll be a full day's walk. I've reserved an albergue for tomorrow night; we need to fully immerse Stu in the pilgrim lifestyle, after all!

Just as we stood waiting for the bus I heard a bunch of people calling my name. To my surprise it was Wes, from Taiwan, and some of the other Taiwanese, South Korean and Malaysian people we have met on our travels. They are such lovely people and it was great to see Wes again. He explained that he'd got the train to León, rested a few days and his foot was now better, so he'll start walking again tomorrow.

Stu has just sent me a message to say he's arrived, which is good news. We've arranged to meet at 7.30 am.

Day 23: León to Hospital de Órbigo

Today has been fantastic and a laugh from beginning to end, aided somewhat by having Stu with us. He also picked a great day to start his Camino.

I introduced Chris and Stu and we all set off walking and chatting, a renewed enthusiasm in the air owing to his arrival. We found a small café on the outskirts of León for some breakfast. What followed was a very long and hot walk over some pretty countryside.

In the afternoon the path had a long line of pylons which ran parallel to it, and it reminded me of the song 'Telegraph Road' by Dire Straits, so I listened to it through my headphones, whilst singing along out loud.

But the highlight of today has to be the last kilometre and the events that followed. As we approached our destination we came across a fantastic long medieval bridge. It was quite something and I decided it was my favourite place so far. Stu certainly was being spoiled on day one.

Dire Straits, 'Telegraph Road'

The albergue I have chosen is very pretty, but it transpires it is a vegan place. It's called Albergue Verde – maybe there was a clue in the name. It's a really beautiful place with wonderful hosts. For dinner, thirty-one of us sat outside and just before we were served gorgeous fresh food we were serenaded by a man with a guitar. It was really quite special.

However, the inevitable happened, and meat-eating Chris became the centre of all jokes. We had to sing a song in Spanish (a type of grace), and Stu and I kept replacing some of the words with 'lamb chops', 'steak', 'hamburguesas' etc. The host also explained that we could have breakfast tomorrow and that there would be rice milk to go with the cereal. At that point Stu exclaimed to Chris, 'Ha, you can't even have the juice of cow!' and everyone collapsed in hysterics.

There was no wine with dinner. It's also alcohol-free here, but I felt like we needed some, particularly as it was Stu's first day. Plus Chris needed to enjoy something. So, after checking with the hosts if it was OK to bring wine into the garden, I quickly dashed to the local petrol station and bought four bottles of wine for the table. It might sound generous; it was less than €8, but everyone seemed to appreciate it.

The fully immersive vegan experience at Albergue Verde

The meal tonight and breakfast had no set price. We were told to donate whatever we felt was appropriate when we leave in the morning. As long as you give from your heart the owners don't mind – magic.

We met a retired Irish couple and they were good entertainment. They said there was a local hotel nearby and offered to buy us a drink. Chris went to bed – he was tired (and probably hungry) – but Stu and I went with them. What was funny was that the hotel served huge burgers, so I walked up to the bar and surreptitiously took a photo of someone's burger; we then sent it to Chris along with the text 'Look what you're missing!'

Everyone is asleep now. We arrived quite late, so all three of us have top bunks and the Camino lullaby has already started. A Canadian lady called Leonel is leading the chorus.

Day 24: Hospital del Órbigo to Astorga

The Camino lullaby was accompanied all night long by the acoustic section al farté! On top of that we had a dog barking outside all night. When we got up this morning the one thing the three of us all agreed on was that the vegan food had started to work its magic and we'd got very little sleep.

It's been great introducing Stu to the Camino. When we spoke on the phone before he came out I told him he'd never be as delighted to see a church as when he's here. He wasn't quite sure why until yesterday afternoon, after about twenty-two kilometres in the sun, when he could just make out the rooftop cross of a church in the distance and shouted, 'I see a church!' The reason for this: where there's a church, there's inevitably a café, which means seats where you can sit down, take your shoes off and rest your feet. Welcome to the Camino, Stu!

Yesterday Stu was ribbing me and Chris for staying in the occasional hotel, saying we were supposed to be living the life of pilgrims. It had only been about five minutes since we'd left our albergue this morning when he hopefully enquired, 'So where are we staying tonight?' He'd had enough of albergues already. Needless to say, I decided that after his initiation ceremony I'd treat the guys to a hotel, and upon the advice of Neil I've booked us into the Hotel Gaudí in Astorga tonight.

As we set off this morning Stu asked about the hymn with the words 'to be a pilgrim' in it. He said it featured at his mum's funeral a few months earlier.

Just chillin', man!

Out of nowhere I sang the whole first verse of 'He who would valiant be' and we all joined in with the heartrending lyrics at the end of the verse, '. . . to be a pilgrim,' much to the delight of some other pilgrims within earshot. They appreciated the singing as they walked along; so they said, anyway.

We walked through undulating hills of eucalyptus forests. Cotton was blowing through the air and gathering on tufts of grass, making the ground look like it was covered in little snowdrifts. We also came across a cool little place with hammocks, so we naturally hung out a bit.

Today's walk was a little more uphill than yesterday's, but we were rewarded with an abundance of scenic views. Stu was still going strong with his virgin Camino legs and was continually striding out in front of me and Chris. 'We'll give him two more days,' we chuckled.

What a surprise Astorga was, and the Hotel Gaudí was equally impressive: picturesque, surrounded by Gaudí's palace and a fabulous cathedral. Still, it feels like we deserve it, and the Camino makes you appreciate life's little luxuries even more!

Once we'd showered we left for a beer. It was encouraging to see that Stu had adopted the beginnings of the pilgrim's limp! This is best described by Chris, who observed that when you see pilgrims walking in front of you in the mornings, you can see the soles of their shoes, but come the end of the day you can't, because their walk has transformed into a little shuffle.

Chris and Stu are sharing a double room and I have a room to myself, for the first time in over three weeks. On top of that, the view is incredible; we are overlooking the square right by the cathedral and palace. I need to bring Lisa here.

Chris has finally decided he needs to lighten his backpack. His toes are becoming painful and he needs to take some of the pressure off his feet.

I laughingly told Stu to pick up Chris' backpack and when he did, he couldn't believe it. 'What the hell have you got in there?' he asked. It was still about sixteen kilos.

I later heard Stu laughing and went into their room to see what the fun was. Chris had got the complete contents of his backpack out on the bed, and as well as the big knife he had dropped onto the table at lunch the other day it transpired he was carrying an additional two large knives! There were no words. We all just laughed.

Tomorrow night we are back in an albergue, but we are hoping to make it in time to be in the one run by the confraternity of St James based in London, where apparently they serve afternoon tea most days. Hopefully they'll still have space by the time we get there, but we have a twenty-one-kilometre walk before that, and most of it is uphill.

In two days' time we cross the highest point of the whole Camino. We can still see some snow on the mountains ahead. I can't wait.

Oh, Chris got a slab of meat tonight, so he was much happier.

Day 25: Astorga to Rabanal

We didn't start until nine thirty because Chris went to the post office to post some kilos back to the US. Stu and I thought it would be rude not to order breakfast in the square while we waited for him.

Once we got going we romped through the first ten kilometres at a pace and then, as the heat rose and our legs got more tired, we slowed. At least

Stu had formally joined the club and was no longer marching off in front of us.

We approached a hamlet called El Ganso, which sounded like Gonzo from the Muppets, so we did the natural thing and sang the theme tune as we walked the final few metres to a café. Shortly after our daily mid-morning ritual of coffee and orange juice we were back on our way.

We all walked alone for a few kilometres, and at one point Stu came up to me and said, 'It's funny, I know this might sound strange, but every now and again I keep thinking there's someone walking with me, wanting to pass on my left side, and whenever I turn round there's nobody there.'

The hairs on the back of my neck went up, goosebumps everywhere. I explained my experiences out here. We exchanged serious glances and just started walking again, silently, lost in our own thoughts. #TSGO!

Before we arrived at our destination, we came across a fence with symbolic, handmade crucifixes hung all over it. They were made out of two sticks and held together between the wire fence structures. It went on and on around bends for about 500 metres. If I said there were thousands of them, I wouldn't be exaggerating. I even made one myself and added to the collection.

Thankfully we managed to get into the British albergue tonight. Our host, Vicky, baked scones and we all had a quintessential afternoon tea. Spiffing! Normally we'd have then found a bar, but the albergue had such a lovely English country-styled garden that we went to a shop, bought some canned beers and sat in the garden. Stu played the albergue house guitar and Vicky came and joined us. It was super chilled.

Following this we went to church, not for mass but for vespers: the local monks performing Gregorian chanting. Stu came. It was quite something. The church was twelfth-century, very simple and plain. It was not pretentious in any way and I really liked it, despite all the cracks everywhere.

As we sat in the church I asked Stu if he'd seen the sign outside that said 'FOR ONE NIGHT ONLY: MONKS UNPLUGGED', and he nearly lost it. My timing was impeccable as it was about fifteen seconds before the chanting began; the church suddenly became silent in anticipation of the performance, leaving us sniggering like two naughty children in a school assembly.

Tomorrow we head up to the Cruz de Ferro (Iron Cross). This is the highest point on the Camino and I know it will be emotional. This is where I'll place the stone I've brought from home at the foot of a tall cross, amongst the many millions that have been laid before. I'm not sure what to expect, but I have a feeling it will mean something and be very spiritual. The monk in church talked about it, stating that it is a special place as it is the closest place to heaven along the whole Camino, and then left it hanging. He had a look on his face that said, *You'll see!*

We're all in top bunks again tonight. The room has ten bunks but there's a bit more space than normal. We seem to know 80% of the people staying here, and they're all good fun, although that doesn't guarantee they won't snore their arses off. Leonel is staying in our room, and if the night in Albergue Verde is anything to go by it's going to be a loud one. Chris is sleeping above her tonight. Here's hoping!

Day 26: Rabanal to Molinaseca

The snoring was so loud last night that Stu downloaded an app in the middle of the night just so that he could record it. He played it to us this morning. The recording included the church bells outside our window, which went off on the hour, but for some bizarre reason chimed again a few minutes after! They stopped at midnight, but the snoring didn't. Stu had the world's loudest snorer underneath him. He was Dutch, and gave Leonel a run for her money. Apparently he hit sixty decibels!

Stu played it again. It was hysterical. He explained that his bunk was shaking with every snore. In a sentence that highlighted just how well Stu was grasping the true pilgrim spirit, he said, 'At one point I seriously thought about grabbing one of Chris's knives and stabbing the guy through the heart!'

That would have made an interesting whodunnit. 'Dutch pilgrim stabbed with American knife in British confraternity hostel in Spain; nobody inside hears anything above the snoring and a backdrop of church bells constantly ringing outside.'

The morning walk was beautiful, warm and clear, and the path was good as it rose up to the Cruz de Ferro. From my research I know it is often cold, windy and wet here, shrouded by cloud. So it was a welcome surprise that today's weather was calm, with clear blue skies. This added to the occasion;

the views on the ascent were fantastic and the colours and scents were amazing.

I had mixed feelings about the cross. I was expecting it to be a solemn, emotional place, which to a certain extent it was. We spent about an hour there, contemplating loved ones, but unfortunately it was too much of a tourist attraction for me. Busloads of disrespectful tourists kept arriving and the ambient noise of their constant chatter ruined the atmosphere for me.

That said, I did get a little bit emotional, not here at the cross, but both on the way up and on the way down.

About three kilometres before the cross I called Lucy to tell her that today was the day I would be placing our stone at the cross. Lucy had chosen the stone with me on Easter Sunday, when I'd had a fantastic day out with all the family, including my mum. Once I'd hung up, I started to think about home and how much I was missing my family. Clutching the stone in my pocket, I became quite tearful.

Contemplation at Cruz de Ferro

When I arrived at the cross, reading some of the messages on the stones was quite sobering. It was a shrine of shrines. The words on each pebble demonstrated the sheer power that the Camino has over people as they memorialised their loved ones at this special place. A few people around me were in tears. Each pilgrim soberly approached the mound of rocks to place their stone, all for different reasons. In the background somebody played Vera Lynn's 'We'll Meet Again'. It added to the occasion.

It was only shortly after we left, when I was reflecting upon the whole experience with Chris, that he told me he was the one who had played the song. He said he only started to play quietly, but two people sitting either side of him started humming along and asked him to turn the music up loud, so he did and chose that moment to place his stone, no doubt full to bursting with thoughts about Karen as he did. The Cruz means different things to different people. I found myself feeling very sad for him.

This afternoon was, however, a nightmare. It was 36°C and was by far the hardest day I've had out here.

Chris started to have trouble with a septic toe, so once we arrived at the village of El Acebo we stopped for a drink. In fact, it seemed to take forever to get there, partly because we were lied to. The fact is that the Cruz de Ferro is *not* the highest point on the Camino; it comes about two kilometres afterwards, at a fairly nondescript hilltop. We weren't expecting this. We thought it would be downhill from the Cruz, but not so; the next hill is fifteen metres higher than the Cruz.

Anyway, after a drink in a local café Chris decided to get a taxi to our destination town of Molinaseca. We had already been walking downhill for about five kilometres and his toe was killing him from the pressure that descending created at the front of his boots.

The driver arrived and put Chris's bags in the back. He turned to me and Stu and asked if we also wanted to get in. Had we known what lay ahead we'd have jumped in without hesitation. In fact, foolishly, not only did we decline; in a typical display of masculinity we declined his second offer, to put our backpacks in the taxi. What a major mistake that was. Our suspicions were raised when the taxi driver just looked at us and said, 'You must be crazy!'

The combination of heat, lack of fluids and the terrain was crippling. A further six kilometres downhill on very rugged, steep and incredibly rough terrain. All in all we descended over 1,000 metres. It took us over three hours to complete it. At one point I looked at Stu and said, 'Why didn't we empty part of our backpacks and put some of the stuff we won't need today in the taxi with Chris?' It wasn't funny, but when you're shattered and dehydrated you just plod on and don't necessarily think straight.

Stu was really struggling now; we both were. I tried to encourage him and lighten the mood; I told him there would be mermaids with ice-cold beers waiting for us in Molinaseca. I think he thought I'd gone delirious.

Then, to make matters worse, we came across one of those pilgrim-taster bus tours, or, to be more accurate, they came across us. When you get people in their seventies with a spring in their step bounding past you, hopping from rock to rock, all with the same little blue backpack just big enough to hold their sandwich box, you know you're struggling. But this group, who happened to be German, had clearly all received instructions from their guide on the minibus about what to do if they encountered a real pilgrim! Every time they walked past us, without fail, one by one they would look up, enthusiastically offer a 'buen Camino' and skip ahead.

The horrible path to Molinaseca

The previous version of me would have been irritated by this, but the now super-chilled, at-peace-with-the-world Simon, who had been on the Camino for twenty-six days, just ignored it and replied with the same phrase, as you do out here.

But they just kept coming, and every time they approached us from behind we had to move to one side to let them past. It was beginning to wear thin. It was tough enough, the path was very narrow and it was painful to move out of the way each time; we just wanted to get there.

I was so knackered that when one unsuspecting Großvater trotted past me, offering his polite 'buen Camino', I replied calmly but firmly with, 'Yeah, buen fuckin' bus ride!'

I don't know where it came from. Stu was part horrified, part hysterical, but was too tired to show either emotion. I just hobbled on, hoping the poor chap didn't understand English!

I looked ahead and could see that the path wound itself down around a sharp corner, where there appeared to be an exit through some undergrowth. It had obviously been trodden down by some previous near-death pilgrims desperate to get off these rugged rocks and onto the smooth surface of the road. I called back to Stu in excitement about what I could see. He didn't even have the energy to acknowledge me.

When I got to Molinaseca there was a little stone bridge over a river. The river banks were green and lying on the grass were myriads of people, many of whom were women in bikinis. I called back to Stu, 'You won't believe this, mate; there's actually mermaids here!'

We just stood looking at the scene in front of us. Not in a lecherous way; just because we had stopped and didn't want to start moving our legs again. We were completely knackered.

We found Chris and our accommodation. The first thing we did was gulp down as much water as our hot bodies could take. It was only about 5 pm, but Stu went to bed.

Chris and I went for a pilgrim meal. The laws of supply and demand are at work out here, as the average price of a pilgrim set meal is increasing each day, the nearer we get to Santiago.

When we got back Stu had left us a little present: the pants and socks that he'd worn today, right on top of the washing machine, which already had a full load of his washing in. He'd obviously put a load in before hitting the sack, but forgotten to put in the ones he was wearing! We did the decent thing: washed them, and hung all his washing out to dry. That's what the Camino does to you. Back home I'd have just left them, but he was a man in need of rest, so handling his sweaty underwear was a necessary act of kindness.

It has been the toughest day yet, certainly one of the hottest, and I'm looking forward to a good night's sleep myself now. I guess we'll go for another stroll tomorrow!

Day 27: Molinaseca to Cacabelos

Stu woke feeling fully recovered. He'd had about fourteen hours' sleep. He then explained that when I had pointed out the exit path to the road yesterday afternoon, he had looked at it and had been in serious doubt that he'd actually make it to the road. I knew he had been suffering; we both had.

We had a cultural morning soaking in the history of the wonderfully preserved Knights Templar castle in Ponferrada. The castle was built in 1178 to protect pilgrims. It is now owned by the king of Spain and is the best castle I've ever been to. It's awesome and we spent a lot of time exploring it before we decided we ought to get moving.

Stu's underwear didn't quite dry overnight, so he pinned his pants to the outside of his backpack, a practice that is commonplace on the Camino. However, he completely forgot as we were walking through the city of Ponferrada with his smalls swinging freely, in full view of everybody walking past. We laughed about how the Camino strips you bare and we couldn't imagine him doing this whilst walking around Worthing.

This afternoon was incredibly hot (38°C in the sun), and unfortunately Chris was still suffering, but this time from a bit of dehydration and an upset stomach. Sadly he decided to make his way to our destination via a taxi again.

Stu and I ploughed on and we loved it. Despite the heat there was quite a lot of shade; we walked through vineyards and forests and lovely rolling countryside. We were listening to our music and eating up the kilometres as we bounded along.

We stumbled upon a guy in a caravan in the middle of a forest, which was a bit of an oasis. As we sat sipping an ice-cold drink we noticed a stream

Stu with his underwear on display in Ponferrada

running by. We dipped our hot and sweaty feet in. Stu said, 'My feet have got ice-cream brain freeze!'

We met up with Chris; he's a bit better but still not feeling great, so we've decided we'll all have a rest day tomorrow. To be honest, it will do us all good. I have walked for twenty-two days on the trot (no pun intended) and the thought of being in the same bed two nights running feels brilliant.

The only downside is that another rest day will likely mean I don't get to Santiago until the Sunday now, but Lisa, being Lisa, was absolutely cool with this when I told her. She said that she and Paula (Stu's wife) will just spend a day chilling in Santiago and that I shouldn't break my neck to get there.

We've done a bit of shopping today too. Stu bought a new wooden staff to help him with his pilgrim's limp (it's pretty cool, actually) and we have all been to the local pharmacy. All three of us walked in and headed for the Compeed section, which, funnily enough, is right by the front door!

Day 28: Rest day in Cacabelos

My feet have loved me today. If they could speak I'm sure they'd have been shouting at the top of their voices, *Thank you for not stomping on me all day in the blistering heat, with that bloody load on your back!*

That said, I have found it a bit tricky to sit still. I've been on the move for so long, that having a rest day, whilst blissful, bizarrely took a bit of adjusting to.

I woke up after ten hours of much-needed sleep. Stu and Chris were still zonked, so I crept out and had an absolutely wonderful leisurely breakfast. I rarely get the time to enjoy breakfast at such a slow pace; it was great.

I went and did some chores afterwards: I got my hair cut, posted a kilo of clothing back home (I'd better warn Lisa, I thought; she might think I've sent her a present!), bought some more sun cream and another disposable razor. It only took forty-five minutes to do the lot!

I then sat in the plaza major (main square), where the guys came and met me. We had a couple of coffees and hot chocolates, watching the world go by, as the temperature steadily rose. I had a couple of lovely telephone conversations with my mum and Lisa, and then we went for a walk to the river; only a short walk, though.

The day rolled into lunch (just some light tapas) and then afternoon beers with the Swiss pilgrim whom Chris and I have met a few times before. She's walking alone, so we invited her to join us at dinner. Afterwards, and rather embarrassingly, none of us could remember her name!

We explored the church and popped back for a siesta, which is where I am right now.

I'm lying on my bed and my thoughts are centred on Chris. He has to make an important decision, and it is one that will impact me too. He went to the medical centre earlier. They checked him out and then sent him to a podiatrist. He's better in himself, but he has a very septic toe. They've dressed it and told him not to walk for two days.

We've just had that difficult conversation: I need to carry on walking so that I can meet Lisa in Santiago. He needs time to decide whether to let me go on my way and continue on his own, or get a taxi for the next couple of days and stay with me.

I tried hard not to influence him and to let him make the decision. It is his

Camino and he has to do what's right for him. If he decided to stay here and rest, it would be difficult to say goodbye to him in the morning, particularly as we've been together for four weeks, but I have to let him decide.

*

Just before dinner Chris casually announced that he's decided to get a taxi to wherever we are walking to tomorrow and that he'll come back next year, or the year after, to complete the bits he's missed. I was delighted. He'd been such a huge part of my journey, and it just wouldn't feel right now if we didn't finish together.

The rest has done us all good. Whilst it means I likely won't get into Santiago until Sunday 9 June now, instead of the eighth, Lisa fully understands. She and Paula will have a great time getting familiar with Santiago anyway. It'll be the eve of Pentecost, so I'm sure two Catholic girls will find plenty of things to get involved in, and if not, there's always gin!

In a funny way, getting in on the Sunday might be better and more romantic – after all, it will be our twenty-ninth wedding anniversary – but it will mean another day without Lisa and I'd really pinned my hopes on being there by Saturday.

Day 29: Cacabelos to Vega de Valcarce

We left Chris just before sunrise today and got a march on. The path meandered alongside a stream as it wove its way through high-sided hilltops, but the countryside was juxtaposed with a huge elevated motorway that we kept traversing underneath. Having such an ugly structure running through the countryside isn't pretty, but it served as a wonderful reminder of life outside the Camino and of how lucky I am to be here, and so free. I listened to the constant drum of lorries and cars passing overhead. I had the pleasure of walking through this serene and beautiful countryside; they were whizzing over it. I knew where I'd rather be.

Because it was Saturday there were lots of local cyclists out, with mini pelotons riding up and down the quiet valley road. I enjoyed watching them, as the riders made the most of the early morning before the heat set in. I thought, *That would be me back home right now, out with my club,* but I was happy to be here, very happy indeed.

Stu and I had completed twenty-six kilometres by 1.30 pm when we bumped into Chris, sitting in the bar immediately opposite our B&B. He'd had a rough night with more upset tummy trouble and his toe was still sore. Unfortunately, I too woke up with an upset stomach, but an Imodium tablet seems to have sorted me out. I'll probably be constipated for the next few days! Hopefully mine will be a one-off, unlike his.

The village we're staying in is very sleepy. It's one street and our accommodation is on the river that we followed all morning. And when I say 'on' I mean we can hear the river from our beds! It did, however, give us the chance to wash our clothes in very fresh and fast-moving water.

There's nowhere to go here other than the river on one side of the building or the bar across the road on the other. It isn't anything at all like Vegas, we joked, but we decided to gamble on spending what was left of the afternoon exploring the bar.

I taunted Chris that even he can't get lost here as it's only fifteen feet from the bar to our accommodation. However, anything could happen after he's had a couple of the local claras.

There was a hilarious moment when I asked the owner of the establishment if he would be showing the Champions League final tonight. Chris said, in his broad Trinidadian accent, 'Oh, yes, is that Tottingham versus Livingpool?' Stu and I just looked at each other and laughed.

Stefan also joined us. He's a happy-go-lucky Swiss guy, always smiling, but whenever we've bumped into him he's been walking in the wrong direction. He's a really funny and, as we were about to discover, really interesting chap. Stu asked him what he did for a living. 'I sell medical marijuana,' he replied, straight-faced. It might explain why he's always so happy.

He bought us a beer, went for a smoke and we agreed to meet up again tonight for the football. The bar becomes the local restaurant in the evening, so we'll eat together too. It's not like there's anywhere else to go.

Also in the bar is a group of young Danish lads whom we've not seen before. They told me they were Premier League fanatics and that they all want 'Tottingham' to win because of Christian Eriksen, the Dane who plays for them. It should be a fun night.

Chris kept looking at his watch. I asked if he was OK, wondering why on earth he would need to keep an eye on the time. He replied with, 'Yes, but a car just went by. I've been timing the traffic. This morning, whilst I was here waiting for you guys, there was a car roughly every five minutes; now, being siesta time, it is every sixteen minutes!' Talk about super chilled.

Day 30: Vega de Valcarce to Fonfría

I woke up to find a couple more people had sponsored me and to my delight I've now raised over £4,000. Rather appropriately, the people to tip me over that figure were Cara and Chris. It gave me a boost, and little did I know how much boosting I might just need today. It was very, very hilly and very, very steep, but I felt fitter than I've felt in about twenty years, so I just enjoyed the fact that I was able to walk and powered up the first big climb to Ocebriero.

I was in my element. I absolutely loved it. I was just bouncing along, eating up the altitude and sweating one out, big time. I felt like I could walk uphill all day.

When I got to the top it was only 10 am and my shirt had the sweat profile of my backpack straps. I waited for Stu and we had a well-earned drink and rest stop. Chris was giving his toe another day off and was going to meet us later.

We soon realised this wasn't the top, nor was it the end of climbing for the day. About two hours later, after more climbing, I joked with Stu that today was the equivalent of going to the gym on a Sunday morning and having a really hard three-hour workout, following which you decide to get back in the gym and do it all again.

The last climb up to the top of Alto do Poio was long and incredibly steep. Lisa called me just as I started to climb it, so she had to put up with my panting and heavy breathing whilst we chatted on the ascent! The scenery has been brilliant and the weather not so hot, which was welcome; it was probably cooled by the altitude.

As I crested, still talking with Lisa, I noticed something: within seconds my breathing and heart rate had returned to normal. My fitness has really improved.

We also moved into Galicia, the sixth and final region of the Camino. We stopped to observe the rather significant boundary marker by the side of the

track and take some photos. At its foot were lots of pebbles and pieces of rock upon which people had written words of encouragement, prayers, names of loved ones etc. One really resonated with me. It had a yellow arrow pointing to the west, and written upon it was a poignant little message: 'The end is a gift. Open it slowly!!'

It stopped me in my tracks. I stood looking at it, and it made me reflect upon how lucky I am to be here. It is hard going at times and I can't wait to get to Santiago now and see Lisa, but there's a danger that my desire to get to the end becomes all-consuming and I forget to enjoy the now. This *will* soon be over; I must take care to ensure I unwrap the last part of this wonderful present *very* slowly. Thank you to whoever placed that stone there.

Fonfría is in the middle of nowhere. Chris doesn't like it because outside it smells of cow dung; in fact we got the faint whiff of it about a kilometre out, and as we neared it grew stronger. We soon saw why. Just one look at this section of the Camino and you could tell that more cows walked along it each day than pilgrims, and it got thicker the nearer we got to the centre.

I say 'centre'; there was a farm building. In fact the whole hamlet is the farm. It reminded me of a phone conversation I'd had with Neil when trying to locate him on his previous pilgrimage. He described where he was staying that night as 'a one-horse town, but where the horse had got up and left'. I think the total population of this hamlet must be no more than thirty; one is the farmer, there's his wife, and the other twenty-eight are cows.

Imagine our surprise when we turned the corner as we wandered through the cowpats and found a modern-looking building nestled into the hillside. There were people sitting outside in the sunshine, or hanging washing on a line; could this be our albergue?

Indeed it was; it was brilliant, too. We did our washing and sat on a sunbed in the garden, enjoying the sunshine, with a deserved glass of vino tinto. Chris tasted it and immediately said he could tell it was a local wine, full-bodied, a certain vintage with a distinct bouquet: 'I'm getting ... I'm getting ... that's it ... cow shit.'

I showered first and sat in the lounge area waiting for the others. Yes, this was a luxurious albergue! As well as having a lounge I spent €1 to have my legs massaged by one of those machines you get in airports. I think this one had been donated because it was broken. It gave me cramp and I jumped off it before it had finished, groaning and hopping about, but it broke the ice between me and some guys who had come to sit in the room.

By the time Chris and Stu appeared I had already had a few glasses of red wine and was enjoying the company of my new friends, who just so happened to be in the British army. Four guys who have walked the Camino a week at a time spanning the last five years. Apparently, they finished at this albergue last year and were now back, this being day one, hoping to finish their pilgrimage this week. We were cracking jokes and the banter levels were high, as you'd expect when you get army boys in town taking the piss out of a little office boy like me. I gave as good as I got, primarily as their military training days were obviously far behind them and a little middle-aged spread, let's say, has got the better of them. It made for a very pleasant and fun evening.

We went for our pilgrim meal in an old round hut: steak, of course, brought out to us by a dancing and singing grandma. You just had to be there. It was made funnier by the fattest guy from the army who, as she was serving dessert, got up and merrily danced with her, a dish of flan still in her hand.

Santiago is now less than 100 miles away. That is such a massive milestone, both psychologically and physically. Amazingly, I also have another new blister. You'd think that, having walked for five weeks, I'd have feet like granite. Oh well, more Compeed.

Santiago seemed like such a distant goal when I started out. I can almost smell it; well, I probably could if it wasn't for the pungent aroma of dung in the air. Even better, Chris is hoping to be walking with us again tomorrow, which will be brilliant.

Day 31: Fonfría to Samos

After the ascents of yesterday, my guidebook suggested that today would be a relatively straightforward twenty kilometres downhill. The weather was cloudier and therefore cooler and the scenery turned into something similar to the Devonshire countryside with rolling hills, low cloud and lush green grass.

Galicia is renowned for being wet and windy and the forecast for the next few days looks like it'll live up to expectations, threatening heavy rain the day after tomorrow. Still, Stu wants to use the waterproofs that he's carried with him for over a week now. His wish might just come true.

The best part of the day was walking with Chris again. He's feeling much better but decided to get a taxi to the bottom of the first hill; it was pretty steep for the first six kilometres and walking downhill isn't the best thing to do when you have a sore toe! We met up in Triacastela and it was great to have him back on the trail. We looked for the three castles. We saw the remnants of one rampart on a hillside, but we couldn't quite be sure and decided they must all be ruined.

Our destination tonight is Samos. It is built around one of the oldest monasteries in the western world. The monastery is a sixth-century masterpiece and incredibly large. We first saw it from up high and could tell it was huge even from a distance, but when we turned the corner and were confronted with the impressive façade we all just stood still, gazing up at its enormity.

At first we thought we might stay in the albergue in the monastery. We were quite excited about it. Stu enthusiastically asked, 'Do I get my own monk?'

As it happens we found a little place over the road. We were a little disappointed initially, but when I read my guidebook out loud to the lads, and they learnt that the monastery has over seventy beds in one long corridor, the guys were suddenly very thankful for our modern little room with its own bathroom.

We lay resting the wrong way round on our beds, with our feet propped up against the wall. It had become a daily ritual to let the blood flow away from our feet.

As we lay there in the vicinity of that vast monastery, we started talking about Easter. Stu explained that every Easter Sunday he and Paula watch *Life of Brian* (religiously!). Chris watches *Jesus Christ Superstar* and *Brother Sun, Sister Moon*. I think I'm somewhere in the middle, but it sums up why I think we're all getting on so well, and the fun we're having: we're all coming at this from completely different angles, and overall it makes for very entertaining conversations.

We decided upon a siesta before our tour of the monastery, which was scheduled for 5.30 pm.

The tour was incredible. The monastery was indeed very grand. It was deceiving too, bigger on the inside. The church within it was a similar size to the huge cathedrals we'd encountered on our travels.

Then our guide explained that the monastery was home to only nine monks.

Nine!

Stu couldn't quite believe it. The accommodation block alone was the size of a small university campus.

That evening we went to find somewhere for dinner and on the way poked our heads into the albergue in the monastery to see what we had missed out on. It was indeed a long corridor of wall-to-wall bunk beds. Worse still, immediately outside the sleeping area is a petrol station, literally built into the walls of the albergue. Honestly, it looked grim and we pitied those who would have to sleep in that long room, inhaling the fumes from outside the door.

Our next task was to avoid being run over. I am sure the monastery was once in a peaceful and tranquil setting, but now huge trucks drive through the village at high speed, to and from the quarry that we saw from high up on the hills before our descent.

We found a cool place for dinner, but every now and again Stu would just come out with one word: 'Nine!' He still couldn't get his head around it.

It also left us pondering: given that there is so much unused space in the monastery, why do they put the pilgrims in the equivalent of a petrol station forecourt shop? Where was the spiritual charity being extended by the monks? All nine of them!

Day 32: Samos to Morgade

Well, it definitely felt like walking through the Devonshire countryside today, because it rained all morning. The good news is Stu got to use his waterproofs. It certainly didn't ruin the morning and we made good progress following a river valley, which wound its way through a forest where the tree canopy was thick enough to shelter us from the worst of the rain.

We then came across a rather cute albergue, run by an elderly couple. They were very sweet and, having served us coffee, chocolates, tortillas, cured meat and a fruit bowl, they couldn't have made us feel any more welcome.

The elderly man spoke English, although, whilst knowing the words, he didn't really know how to pronounce them, so it was very difficult to understand what he was saying. That said, it didn't stop him trying; he continually talked to us for the whole forty-five minutes we were there.

We managed to piece together that the lady in the kitchen was not his wife, but they had been together for seventeen years and had recently decided to turn the cottage into an albergue: 'To give us something to do,' as he put it. It transpired that the albergue had only been open for three days, although the old man had lived there for many years.

Chris commented on how amazing the cured ham was. The man explained it was his own pig, which he killed in December, put in a box in the ground and later dug up and hung in the attic. 'It gets exposed to the north wind, which is the best wind for curing ham,' he informed us! It seemed to work; it was delicious. As you can guess, Chris now seems to be well over his tummy bug. He still blames eating salad!

A few other pilgrims also trying to get out of the rain joined us. One asked the man if there was any Wi-Fi, to which he replied, 'There is no Wi-Fi downstairs.'

My curiosity got the better of me, so I asked him if there was Wi-Fi upstairs. He looked quite peculiarly at me, then began ranting in his dreadful English, but we had no idea what he was saying. It certainly seemed to have nothing to do with Wi-Fi, and we just looked at each other, a bit bemused, wondering what I had said to make him appear so angry.

It was only when I managed to work out that he was talking about cancer and occasionally saying 'esposa' (the Spanish word for 'wife') that the penny dropped. He thought I'd asked if his wife was upstairs! It took some unravelling, as she'd died of cancer many years ago, and he had become animated because he wondered why I thought he would have a woman in the kitchen whilst his wife was upstairs. Stu, Chris and the other pilgrims were in stitches. Thankfully our host eventually saw the funny side of it too.

The lady in the kitchen appeared. I told her that I really enjoyed the Spanish omelette, and before I could stop her she went back to the kitchen to make me some more! It was good, though.

When I asked for the bill the lady pointed to a sign on the wall. It said, in English, 'Donation only'. Incredible! I suppose it prevents you from having to work out a price list or print a menu; life is simple out here.

We reached the large town of Sarria around lunchtime. This is the last place where you can start your Camino to Santiago as it is just over 100 kilometres from Santiago and therefore entitles you to a compostela: the official certificate of completion. It therefore is the point where the Camino gets very busy as lots of people start their pilgrimage from here.

Whilst I accept that not everybody will be able to walk for 500 miles, and that walking from Sarria will be as much of a challenge for them as my Camino has been for me, there are clearly some people who are just along for the ride. This has given rise to a new term amongst the three of us: 'filgrim' (fake pilgrim), and we amuse ourselves every time we see them, with Chris commenting on their lack of a suntan, limp or odour, normally followed by us playing and singing along to the Proclaimers' 'I'm Gonna Be (500 Miles)' as they come bounding past us, fresh-legged and full of energy. It keeps us entertained.

Sarria isn't very pretty. It has outgrown itself, probably due to the volume of pilgrims who start from here and walk through it. It's a concrete conurbation and, from the aroma in the streets, the sewage system was not built to cope with this many people.

On the plus side, there was a lot of graffiti: not the sort daubed on trains and sides of buildings in the UK, but proper, brilliant street art. It was as though Banksy had once completed the pilgrimage and, whilst he hugged the statue of St James in Santiago, a voice had spoken to him: *You must go back to Sarria and daub images of your pilgrimage on the walls of the city to cheer the place up.* They were everywhere and they certainly helped. And yes, your imagination runs away with you out here.

We were expecting huge crowds after Sarria, but no. I think the fact that we didn't get there until lunch meant that the filgrims would have already left for the day, plus it was another hot one. The forecast for tomorrow is, however, typically Galician, with serious rainfall expected, so we made hay whilst the sun shone, or something like that.

We walked twenty-five kilometres today. Tomorrow is more undulating than today and will be a considerably tougher day, given the forecast. The good news is that Chris's foot is better and, if we manage to walk twenty-seven kilometres to Ligonde tomorrow, we might even be in with a chance of making it to Santiago for Saturday – 'the end is a gift, open it slowly' still at the front of my mind.

We booked into a hostel tonight. We've discovered that most of the accommodation between here and Santiago has already been booked in advance, owing to the large volume of pilgrims, so chances are the better albergues are all full. As it happened, we got lucky and tonight we have a private, interconnected two-bedroom apartment with a shower in each room. One is a double and the other a twin. Stu has bagged the double and isn't moving from it. He's even christened it his 'wankarium'!

When the owner asked us if we wanted dinner it wasn't as though we could walk to a nearby restaurant, so we obviously signed up! It's a peaceful and quiet place, to say the least.

Having passed the '100 miles to go' point a couple of days ago, we should pass the significant '100 kilometres to go' marker early tomorrow morning. You'll remember I included the same landmark in my poem, so it will be great to see it for real and reflect on my achievements thus far.

Right on cue we met a couple of filgrims at dinner. Actually, they were lovely ladies: cousins, in fact, from Vancouver, and the elder was seventy. We soon spotted that they were filgrims; it was revealed just after a phone call I made to book an albergue for Thursday night. The younger lady leaned over to us and enquired, 'Excuse me for interrupting, but I overheard your conversation and you mentioned the word "albergue". We've seen that word around a lot; what does it mean?'

The three of us simultaneously burst out laughing. We then felt a bit guilty, so we politely explained why. I told them the word 'pilgrim' has got the word 'grim' in it for a reason, and surmised that they were therefore only on a 'pilage'! They took it all in good humour.

As I hung my washing out tonight with my peg, I developed a theory about pegs on the Camino. When I was at that albergue in Orisson, desperate to find one, there were none; they were like gold dust. But now, as we're nearing Santiago, people no longer need their pegs, so they just take their washing off the line and leave them for others. All of a sudden, there are plenty to choose from. I think all the pegs actually follow the Camino too, starting in St Jean and, over time, getting carried by different pilgrims as they make their way towards Santiago. I am keeping mine. I've become quite attached to it, and I'm taking it home as a souvenir.

Day 33: Morgade to Ligonde (Monterosso)

We set off early again, and again it was raining. I even wore my poncho. Might as well use it; I've carried it for over four weeks. Though, looking at tomorrow's forecast, it might be out again.

We arrived at the '100 kilometres to go' marker and stopped for some photographs. We didn't hang around though, because it was raining hard.

We ploughed on silently. Silent insomuch as we didn't speak, as we had our hoods right up and heads down to keep the wind from blowing rain into our faces, but noisy as the rain battered against our hoods.

In fact, the driving rain was so bad that we found we'd wandered off course. We'd obviously missed a sign when we'd had our heads down. We quickly worked out a way to rejoin the Camino, and by our rough calculations figured it would add another two kilometres to today's walk. We just accepted it and ploughed on; what's another two kilometres in the grand scheme of things? There'd be no benefit in complaining or blaming anyone.

We rejoined the Camino just before we descended to a large reservoir, and then crossed a very long bridge towards a pretty-looking town called Portomarín. At the end of the bridge stood a large flight of steps into the

The '100 kilometres to go' marker

town, and the nearer we got the bigger they looked. We were hoping we didn't have to walk up them, but then we noticed the little yellow Camino arrow just to the right of them, pointing left, at the steps. Bugger.

We headed through the town, but we couldn't see any directional arrows for the Camino, which is unusual given there are normally more arrows in the towns. We were lost again! It rained harder too, so we found a café in the town for some shelter and to work out where we'd gone wrong.

We then deduced that the arrow at the very bottom of that large flight of steps had been strategically placed to the right of the steps, pointing left, to entice pilgrims into walking up them and entering the town to spend their money. It had worked on us! Had the arrow been placed to the left of the steps, it would have been plainly obvious to any pilgrim (even ones without any sense of direction, like Chris) that the path went left and there was no need to climb those bloody steps after all.

The misleading arrow up the steps!

The hardest part of the afternoon was getting our clothing right. We wasted so much time putting waterproofs or warm layers on and taking them off, as one minute it was a windy downpour and the next it was sunny and hot.

As I crested one summit a young woman from Belgium walked past me. We walked together for a while and we got on really well. She was an anaesthetist, had started, like Stu, in León and was walking alone. She was a very fast walker. I tried to keep up with her, but I felt I was holding her back.

After a few kilometres we came across a small café and I said, 'It's been a pleasure chatting with you, but I ought to wait for my friends.' The reality was that I needed a rest! Still, there was some truth to my excuse. I had no idea where Stu and Chris were; I had left them behind in my attempt to keep up with Evelyn.

I was pleasantly surprised when Evelyn stayed for a drink too. I introduced her to the boys once they arrived about fifteen minutes later. Evelyn then bid us 'buen Camino' and walked ahead, leaving us old boys to walk at our own, slower pace.

You discover new things every day on the Camino. Today I discovered that my right shoe is no longer fully waterproof! I guess after 600 or so kilometres one can expect perhaps a little wear and tear in a shoe. The good news is the left one is fine, so I decided to concentrate on that and be thankful both feet weren't getting wet.

We covered over twenty-eight kilometres today, excluding our detours for getting lost. We'd started walking at 7.30 am and didn't get to our accommodation until about 5 pm, and given the conditions it had been a full-on day. We were tired and tomorrow we decided we'd try to get to Ribadiso.

Day 34: Ligonde to Ribadiso

We knew that if we made it to Ribadiso tonight we'd definitely make it to Santiago on Saturday, so that was motivation enough to get us through what looked like about thirty-four kilometres. Even better, the rain that was forecast this morning never arrived.

We had a late lunch in Melide, a town famous for its pulpo á feira (boiled octopus). In fact, despite being inland every restaurant seemed to sell it. We were just pleased places were still open. We were worried siesta time may have kicked in, given our long morning's walk. We found a busy place and settled down for some rest and to savour some of the local fresh octopus with chilli; it was gorgeous.

After lunch, we only had 12.5 kilometres to do, but we were hampered somewhat by a deluge of biblical proportions. The promised rain arrived in the promised land, albeit some four hours later than expected. It was so bad that we took very few photographs; we didn't dare get our phones out. In fact the only time a photograph was taken was when we stopped for a quick break under a canopy so I could change my wet socks and tape up my feet to prevent more blisters. It was great to put on fresh dry socks, but I knew, without doubt, they would be soaked within minutes of leaving. Yes, both shoes are no longer waterproof!

Somewhere above the clouds we could hear the occasional jet engine on the flight path to Santiago and we started to feel excited about getting near

Both shoes leaked!

our final destination. Martyn called me, and I really enjoyed talking with him. We also had a very sincere moment. I won't go into detail, but it meant a lot and it sums up why he's such an awesome friend.

We arrived at our albergue tonight and were greeted, unusually, by a very grumpy-looking lady on reception. She then showed us to our room, which looked like a prison cell, and the mattresses looked at least thirty years old.

The three of us looked at each other and I said to the others, 'Shall I wander to that place that we passed on the way in and see if they've got any vacancies?' I didn't get any resistance!

As I walked down the road I uttered a little prayer: 'Dear Lord, if you really are there, please let them have vacancies. It's been a long day; we're soaked and shattered.'

You should've seen the look on the boys' faces when I walked back into the prison cell and said, 'Pick up your bags, boys; we're leaving this shithole.' I even got a refund on the way out.

The owner of our now-lovely hostel even offered to remove our washing from the machine and put it in a tumble dryer whilst we went over the road to get some dinner. Now that is more like service.

Dinner was with Evelyn, the pilgrim from Belgium I met yesterday, who was surprised to see we had walked this far. Not bad for us old blokes, we joked. She's a good laugh but, rather strangely, she drinks red wine with Coke!

We assessed our progress. We've walked in excess of 100 kilometres in the last four days, which is not a small achievement by any standards. The better news is, as a result, we've only got two more days left of circa twenty kilometres each. I will definitely be unwrapping the last two days slowly.

Day 35: Ribadiso to O Pedrouzo

There's been a different spirit on the Camino today, a sense of euphoria and a spring in everyone's step, because for most people today is their penultimate day. We've exchanged 'buen Camino's as per usual, but there is more gusto behind the reply today, frequently followed by a 'nearly there' or 'not far now'. Today, like most days really, has been about the people you meet more than the walk itself, which has been relatively flat and through forests.

We tried to dodge the rain again, pretty successfully, by stopping for coffee whenever it looked like it might just pour down. I could see a huge storm cloud building in the sky to the north of us and told the guys it looked like it was heading our way and that it might be a good time to grab a spot of lunch soon. We walked faster, motivated by the grey cumulonimbus cloud forming ahead, until we stumbled across a little café and managed to get inside just in time to miss a massive hailstorm.

Afterwards, Stu went to pay the bill and came back with shots: 'On the house, apparently!' The owner of the establishment had insisted, and then stopped us just as we were about to leave. He grabbed a lighter, a candle and something that looked like a stamp. He melted some wax onto our pilgrim passports and placed the stamp to create a rather special wax seal. This was followed by handshakes and heartfelt best wishes for our impending safe arrival into Santiago. It doesn't take much to have an impact on someone's day.

My pilgrim passport, with the wax seal and space for the final two night's stamps.

I called Mum just before we got into the town tonight and had a conversation with her that will stay with me forever. It meant the world to me.

The owner of the place we're staying in tonight gave us such a lovely warm welcome and then, when he realised Chris and I had started from St Jean, he got very animated about it. He'd walked from St Jean himself before, so he knew what we'd achieved, but he clearly usually gets filgrims staying here, given we're only nineteen kilometres from Santiago. He was *very* effusive. He came bounding out from behind his counter to embrace us, smiling, welcoming; there was a kindred spirit. It was a lovely moment and one that really brought it home that we're actually nearly there.

Talking of filgrims, there have been plenty, but my favourite was a woman who we bumped into at lunch; she left just as we entered the café where we got the wax seal. She was wearing lots of make-up and a transparent plastic poncho that only reached her waist. Underneath the poncho was a Gucci handbag – seriously? About three minutes later the hail came down; I'd have loved to see her reaction, and we all giggled about it.

Tonight, we had an impromptu mini celebration. We bumped into Stefan, again walking in the wrong direction! He had treated himself to a decent hotel and he invited us to join him for dinner.

First, though, we went to mass in a beautiful church where behind the altar was the largest scallop shell I had seen on the whole walk. It was like something out of a movie set, but somehow seemed fitting given the proximity of this church to Santiago.

The meal was steak and red wine, and it was delicious. The evening was filled with laughter as we retold stories of the last few weeks and more seriously discussed how we might feel tomorrow, as we enter Santiago.

So, we're nearly there. One more night of living out of a backpack and repacking it to walk to a different bed. Four nights in Santiago with Lisa, starting tomorrow, and I simply can't wait. I've had a fantastic time – the Camino is special and hasn't disappointed one bit, the people are brilliant and the spirit is wonderful – but I've really missed Lisa and can't wait to see her now. Lots of our friends are asking me to take photos of our reunion, but that's going to be tricky because all I'm intent on doing is hugging the hell out of the person I care about more than anything. I've envisaged that moment so many times out here, and I can't wait.

I think we'll be skipping to Santiago.

Day 36: Arrival in Santiago

Stu was complaining even before we left because I opened the window last night, as it was so hot. The problem was our hostel was on a busy main road, so he didn't get much sleep, owing to the traffic.

That said, once the realisation of the day had dawned on us, that we'd be at our final destination by mid-afternoon, that was all soon forgotten. We grabbed breakfast in a little café next door and started the last leg of our pilgrimage.

I thought back to the stone that I had seen on the border of Galicia and reflected on just how true the words were: 'The end is a gift. Open it slowly!'

On one hand I didn't want this to end. I've had the time of my life. The headspace, the laughs, the camaraderie, even the tears all make the Camino a magical place.

Yet on the other hand it had been five weeks since I'd seen Lisa. Better still, I knew we had a half-decent hotel room booked for the next four nights. Being in the same bed for four nights in a row is going to be incredible, and with Lisa too. I had my own little gift waiting to be unwrapped (metaphorically, of course) and I simply couldn't wait!

We had a real skip in our step this morning. I was very mindful about being sensitive to Chris, as Stu and I would see our wives waiting for us and clearly he wouldn't. That said, getting to Santiago is going to be pretty euphoric in itself, so I'm sure he'll be fine.

At 8.40 am, after about an hour of walking, Stu and I received simultaneous text messages. Due to a ridiculously early flight, Lisa and Paula were already at Santiago airport. We could actually hear the rumblings of the odd aeroplane engine from the airport, way off to the west, and that seemed to make us walk even faster.

To be honest, I don't remember much about the walk itself today. What I do recall is the following:

1) Stopping for coffee thinking we'd got about five kilometres to go, only to be told by the waiter that it was still another nine or ten kilometres.

2) Removing the cellophane wrapper from Lisa's anniversary card to write it. I had left it on to keep it as clean as I could, but I didn't want to be writing it tonight! I borrowed a pen from a man at a stall by the side of the road; he then realised what I was doing, so he went round the stall and found a little silver shell-patterned heart. He dripped a bit of wax onto my card and stuck the heart to it; it was a lovely touch.

3) Walking around the airport. The path went north of it, and it seemed to take forever to get to Mount Joy, about five kilometres from Santiago. Here we got our first glimpse of the famous cathedral down in the valley. A ripple of excitement grew amongst us, as it did with all the other pilgrims who realised that they were nearly there. Stu cried.

The aptly named Mount Joy

4) Reaching the outskirts of the Santiago and walking for what seemed like forever in suburbia, to the famous archway that led to the square, where I knew Lisa would be waiting. 'Just a few more metres now …' It felt great to be thinking in metres, and no longer kilometres.

I spotted her at the bottom of the steps. She looked amazing, smiling, gorgeous and radiant. She just stood there, resisting the urge to run towards me in order to allow me to finish the last few steps of my journey.

I turned to Chris and Stu and pointed. 'There they are; let's walk in together.'

Chris just smiled at me and said, 'Go on, man,' which was incredibly decent of him.

It was quite a moment.

After the best hug of my life I looked at Chris and Stu; we were all in tears. We embraced, crying tears of joy, of relief, and just of 'thank God it's all over'. We looked up at the splendour of the cathedral through blurred vision, full of unbridled joy. We all hugged each other again; we took photos, took some more and hugged even more. Lisa took a photo of our feet and walking sticks, which turned out to be a real corker.

Our mode of transport!

I can't begin to explain how good it felt just to hold my girl again. I didn't want to let go

Sheer joy!

Shortly after, Evelyn appeared. She had finished her Camino yesterday and just happened to be walking through the square when she noticed us. We also bumped into Stefan, so we all arranged to meet in the square for dinner and a proper celebration tonight. That said, we all ploughed into a local tapas restaurant anyway, to have a well-earned late lunch and to start the celebrations early.

When we got to our hotel I discovered that Martyn and Louise had sent a bottle of champagne to our hotel room. Awesome. It would have been rude not to drink that too!

CHAPTER SIX

Santiago

That evening we met in the square, as planned, and it was great to have clean and fresh clothes on. Lisa had brought out the ones I had packed the day before I left home.

Dinner was glorious. It was a big celebration with some great people and couldn't have gone any better if we'd planned it months in advance.

We'd arranged to meet up with Stefan, Evelyn and Chris, and I took delight in trying to show off my Spanish by calling a few of Santiago's finest restaurants. Most were fully booked, not surprisingly, but one offered me a table and they told me it was free within fifteen minutes. As it happened it

Celebrations! Evelyn, me, Lisa, Stu, Paula, Chris and Stefan

was a private room at a wonderful restaurant with excellent food. There were caring staff to look after us, and they did just that. Stefan was on good form and the wine and champagne flowed.

In fact it was like that for three days. Wherever we went we seemed to drink champagne and eat tapas; it just arrived, normally orchestrated by Chris secretly buying it in the background.

Despite the celebrations, I woke very early the next morning and it took me a moment to realise where I was, and, more importantly, that I wouldn't have to pack up my things and get my walking boots on. Lisa was flat out, a combination of the very early flight and the alcohol. So I quietly got dressed and crept out to get my compostela from the pilgrim's office. I had mentioned the night before that I might do this, just so she'd know where I was when she woke, and despite it being our wedding anniversary!

I had to cross the square to get to the pilgrim's office, and boy, what a contrast it was to the hustle and bustle from the day before. It was completely empty.

I gazed up at the huge façade of the cathedral against the clear blue morning sky, the sun rising behind the building, whilst I stood smack bang in the middle of the square. It was a *very* special moment for me. I cried; well, I sobbed, actually, I couldn't quite believe I'd done it. I had twenty minutes to myself contemplating what I had just achieved, and how many others before me had done the same.

Today's pilgrims started to arrive in the square. It was now 7.30 am, so they had obviously got up at the crack of dawn to be here at this time. I watched them. Some just sat, some walked straight through to the pilgrim's office, some cried and some looked lonely, but I know one thing: they had all been on a journey, a journey that would most likely change them forever. After all, this walk is definitely more about the journey than the destination.

I queued outside the pilgrim's office. I knew I wouldn't qualify for the free lunch at the salubrious fifteenth-century Parador hotel that is offered to the first ten pilgrims each day. I was happy with that. The Camino spirit was alive within me; I'd rather it be given to more deserving pilgrims, some who perhaps would never usually be able to afford to eat in such a prestigious place.

In the afternoon we went to join the queue of people waiting at the cathedral to hug the statue of Santiago (St James) situated at the top of some steep steps at the back of the altar. It felt only fitting to do this, and I was delighted Lisa came with me. I didn't feel moved or anything profound, but I was glad I did it. What was more moving for me was the small crypt underneath the statue where the remains of St James are held in a casket, allegedly. After all, he was one of Jesus' disciples.

Lisa and I then found a cosy little bar and sat talking, just happy to be with each other. It was, after all, our anniversary.

The following day Lisa and I got a taxi to Cabo Fisterra with Chris, Stu and Paula. This is the coastal endpoint of the Camino, the place that was once thought to be the end of the world. It was another eighty kilometres away and, funnily enough, we didn't fancy walking there, but on the way we saw many pilgrims who were.

I spent quite a lot of time sitting on the rocks, looking out to sea, sometimes with Lisa, sometimes alone, reflecting on the past few weeks and wondering how they would change me. There was a part of me that was sad it was all over, but in a way I knew my pilgrimage was only now truly about to start.

Stu got a tattoo of the Camino shell on his ankle. He and Paula were goading me to do the same. I didn't. I opted for a silver shell on a chain, to remind me of my time here each day that I put it around my neck. We also managed to squeeze in afternoon tea at the Parador.

My legs have started to recover, but I am still showing signs of that pilgrim limp even after three days of rest.

The next day Lisa and I went to mass in English, where I did something very unusual. It was not premeditated, but when a nun came out just before mass started and asked the congregation for a volunteer to do a reading, my hand shot up. It just felt like the right thing to do and I knew Lisa would be proud of me, if a little astonished.

Also, before mass started, we all had to stand up and introduce ourselves and say where we had started walking from. I took pride in saying I'd walked from St Jean, and was amazed by how few other people had actually walked from there. Lisa was embarrassed; she had to stand up too, and, obviously only having walked from our hotel to the cathedral, she had some explaining to do!

I'm pretty confident with public speaking, so I enjoyed the reading. It felt like a fitting way to end my Camino.

Afterwards there was a little gathering in a room upstairs. I asked Lisa if we could go to what I jokingly called 'Bible studies'. It worked out a treat because it gave everyone the chance to share their experiences and what they'd gained from their Camino. This was brilliant, and enabled Lisa to witness the profound impact that the Camino had had on so many different people in so many different ways. I loved having her here with me to experience some of its magic.

When it was my turn to speak I said that I only wished that the spirit of the Camino could be taken back by everyone who walks it, to be sprinkled through love and affection on our fellow human beings around the world. To a certain extent I thought, *I hope that's what my book does.*

Lisa and I had an incredibly joyous time in Santiago. We never left the old town, and were just happy to be together. We revelled in the history and sanctuary of the place, and each other, of course. I felt at peace here. Santiago is the happiest city on earth. It was uplifting.

The final evening was another celebration, but I knew that it would be difficult to say goodbye to Chris. I know we'll stay in touch, and I know we'll see each other again – that's a given – but I also know that with a very early flight tomorrow morning we'll have to go our separate ways tonight.

We embraced, cried; he looked sad. We were delighted we'd met each other; we'd shared so much together. Those memories would never leave us. Hasta luego, amigo.

CHAPTER SEVEN

Reflections

During my time in Santiago I often found myself reflecting on the past five weeks.

Interestingly, I had not spent any time thinking about my fathers. In fact, it was only through reading back through these notes that I reminded myself that I had expected to perhaps find room to think more about this. I had the room, I had lots of headspace to do so, but the simple fact of the matter is I didn't.

I now have my own family; I am a father and proud of the fact that I have already been a better father to my boys than any of mine were to me. The only time I really ever think about it is when Mike or James come to the pub with me, something that I always cherish. I hope they appreciate it in a way that I would have appreciated being able to visit the pub with my father, as it was something I was never able to do. I love it more when they buy a round, though!

I did, however, find myself contemplating whether I was the best father I could be, and identified small things that I will do to be an even better dad to both Mike and James. We never stop learning.

One totally unexpected thing that did happen is that I became even closer to my mum. We spoke pretty much every day. We shared some great moments together. It felt like she was walking it with me and I know she enjoyed getting my daily updates. Quite simply, I felt closer to Mum during these past five weeks than at any other moment in my life. #TSGO!

I reflected on the physical achievement. I still can't believe I've accomplished walking 500 miles. I'm not sure the exercise regime would have met the stringent demands of the 'marginal gains' philosophy that's brought incredible success to British cycling:

Step 1:   Drink three to four glasses of red wine every evening.

Step 2:   Go to bed in an uncomfortable and rickety bunk so you have a disturbed night, preferably from snoring, church bells or both.

Step 3:   Wake very early, before it is light. Eat dry bread and, if you're lucky, some jam.

Step 4:   Grab a bottle of water, carry a pack on your back and walk all day in blistering heat with, if you're lucky, a slice of tortilla and a coffee mid-morning. Hope you don't get the shits or a sickness bug.

Repeat for thirty-six days.

And if you manage to do all of this whilst avoiding bedbugs, you're a real winner!

But it works. It worked for me, and works for so many others. The human body is amazing.

Has it brought me closer to God? Don't get me wrong, I'm not going to be running to church each Sunday, but I have definitely got a stronger belief in my faith. I am no longer afraid of entering churches either; in fact I have learned to accept them. The next time I enter a church my mind will immediately flash back to the many places of worship I encountered on the Camino and, instead of looking around in bewilderment, I will use it as an opportunity to practise what I did there. I will embrace the opportunity for quiet contemplation, reflection and appreciation for the love I have in my life. I will even give thanks to my god. If nothing else, churches are an escape from everyday life, and this alone should not be underestimated.

I also found myself pondering the following: *Would I do it again, and, if so, would I do anything differently?* The first part was easy to answer, the second less so.

I simply wouldn't hesitate to walk it again. Maybe not next week, or any time soon; my legs and body need to recover. But I absolutely intend to undertake this incredible journey again and relive its magic, the spirit, the people.

I would, however, perhaps do some things differently. Although it was the most fantastic way to finish my walk by meeting Lisa in Santiago, next time I wouldn't hold myself to a deadline. It was great to have the challenge, but I am now of the belief that you should let the Camino take as long as it takes.

I would relish every footstep all the more, even the painful ones, and enjoy each day, even the boring ones. I would ensure I relished the privilege of yet another day of being able to walk on the Camino. There were some days when I couldn't wait to get to my destination, almost wishing the day away. Each day is a blessing. It would be incredible to walk it with Lisa.

Chris has been talking about coming back to complete the sections he missed towards the end of next year. He's even talking about doing an even longer Camino from Le Puy in France. I can't let him do it all on his own, now can I?

*

It felt strange walking back through my front door. The Crokes had gone to town decorating my house with banners, and there were a few bottles from friends and family to celebrate with.

It also felt very weird being back in the confines of four walls. I find myself wanting to keep going outside, even if just into my garden.

I'm noticing the very small things: flowers budding, birds tweeting and the warm British breeze on my skin. I'm in a very happy place. I have learned to embrace the freedom, the air, the beauty in each day and, more than ever, the ability to 'live in the now'.

The day after arriving home I remembered I'd taken a photo of the soles of my shoes before the start of the Camino, so I grabbed them to see whether they looked very different now, and took another photo.

Before

After

PART 3

After

CHAPTER EIGHT

Post-Camino

Given everything that I've done, my sabbatical is only six weeks old. I still have plenty of time away from work and I have lots of things planned, but also lots of downtime to fill with whatever I want to.

Ascot races

As a rather fabulous early fiftieth birthday present, Martyn and Louise took us to Ascot for the day. Our mutual good friends Steve and Andrea also joined us. It was a day for pomp and circumstance, for getting dressed up in top hat and tails and drinking champagne. And what a contrast it was to the life I had been living only a week or so earlier.

Oh, and, by the way, the trousers fit perfectly around my waistline!

A holiday with my in-laws

Most people would vomit at the thought of having a week away with their in-laws, but not me. Furthermore, it was great to have the time to enjoy another trip, this time to Devon, and the chance to get in some golf. One goal I have this year is to get round my local golf course in less than 90. That's not brilliant, but I only started playing about six years ago and don't really get much time to practise. I've had a few lessons and I've improved from going round in 122 (yes, you read that correctly) to 92 on a good day.

Roger and I played golf every day on different courses. Better still, all four of us could meet up for lunch and dinner, and we got to play snooker and other games in the evenings. We're a family that likes playing games, and it was great to be able to dedicate a complete week to spending some quality time with them.

Lisa and I went to have dinner with Ami, Laurel and Clare. They all live in Devon and we arranged to have a Camino reunion at Ami's lovely cottage. It was a very special evening and demonstrates how strong the bonds that you form on the Camino are, considering I was only with them for the first week.

We also video-called Chris. Needless to say the 'running of the goats' story from Pamplona reared its ugly head.

Mum

I booked in a week to stay with my mum. There were lots of jobs that needed doing as she no longer has a 'man about the house' to help her. She worked me hard! It was a fun but very busy week where I did everything from refelting her shed to chopping down ivy to mending windows.

We did find time for a lovely day on the Dudley canals, where we took a barge through the tunnels, following which I treated her to afternoon tea. Mum managed to get herself locked out of the restaurant, which proved to be quite a comical moment as she was waving at me through the glass and I pretended I couldn't hear what she was saying.

Le Tour de France

Jay and I always try to go and watch a day or two of Le Tour when we get the chance. We've been to the Alps and last year we went to Brittany. This year we were going to two places in France: Provence and then up to the Alps.

Jay and I decided to keep down costs we would go camping. He said he had a big tent and he had practised erecting it with his son Nikul some weeks earlier.

Unfortunately, the conditions in his garden did not exactly emulate the experience of the pretty and quiet campsite in Provence. For example, he had not had to deal with the fact that we had hardly slept the night before due to a very rough ferry crossing. All we could hear from our cabin were car alarms going off every few minutes as the bow crashed into another wave.

Further, we'd been in the car for eight hours and when we were shown to our pitch it was 35°C. There was a Dutch couple opposite us, sitting in the sun, chilling out with a beer on the terrace of some elaborate erection that looked like it had been purchased from the caravanning and camping show.

But the real killer was the fact that the ground was rock hard, and Jay had little aluminium tent pegs and a little metal hammer. They were going nowhere!

After we'd bent about ten pegs, Jay was getting annoyed with himself. 'We didn't have any trouble putting this up in my garden.'

It was the first time I had ever seen Jay sweat so profusely, to the point where his beige shorts had changed colour to a dark brown. We just laughed, as we so often do. We looked like we'd been to a sauna fully clothed.

We looked around in desperation at the flapping canvas lying in a mess, with no way to get the thing secure.

The Dutch guy opposite came over to us and said, 'Here, I can't bear it anymore; please drink these!' and handed us two beers. That made us laugh even more. Jay doesn't drink beer, but he didn't want to be rude, so he put the can behind my car. I *had to* drink both. They didn't last long.

The Belgian chap next door then came to our aid. He popped his head over the privet to enquire when we were leaving. I replied light-heartedly with, 'We've only just arrived; have we pissed you off that much already?'

He chuckled, but when I explained we were leaving on Wednesday he said, 'Hang on,' and disappeared inside. He then presented us with some heavy-duty stakes and a huge mallet, which he said we could use, because he would still be here past Wednesday.

It only took us about another hour to erect the tent and afterwards we needed a dip in the pool to cool down. We decided to go to the local town, Vaison-la-Romaine, for dinner, partly because we were hungry, partly through embarrassment.

We laughed and recounted the events of the afternoon over dinner. We always have a ball. Here we were, less than twenty-four hours in France and we'd already been in hysterics. Further still, we reckoned that our new neighbours think we are a couple, so we decided to play up to it. When we returned, we left the tent to walk to the shower block holding hands, swinging them freely.

As it turned out they were fabulous neighbours; we even watched Le Tour come through Vaison together. We all got on very well, and when, a few days later, we showed them photos of our wives, they were surprised and laughed at the fact that we had camped up our camping.

The day before the tour came through I attempted to cycle up Mont Ventoux. This time I took the route from Malaucène, from the north, as opposed to the traditional Bedouin route that I had done with Jimbo about five years earlier. It was roasting hot and there was little shade. I had to ask some people for water on the ascent, as I was very dehydrated. I did it, but it was hard going. My summit was perfectly timed with a flyby of a Typhoon Eurofighter performing aerial stunts over the top of the mountain, which added to the occasion. The descent was fast, to say the least.

We then drove to the Alps, where we cycled up the Col d'Izoard, and the following day watched the race come past, much slower than they did in Vaison, as the riders were climbing the enormous Col du Galibier.

We love the Tour so much. Some people can't understand why you would stand on a roadside for four hours just to watch some bikes come past when it is all over and done with quite quickly. Well, let me tell you, the atmosphere beforehand is always something special. Wherever we've been it's always been brilliant, and this year was no exception.

Cycling the South Downs Way

This is one adventure I've always wanted to do and, given it was pretty much on my doorstep, I decided that I could build this into my sabbatical. My brother-in-law Chris said he'd do it with me. He came to my house and we planned a gentle four days to cycle the 108 miles over the Downs, which included a night over in Hampshire, a night at home (Worthing is pretty much halfway along the route) and a night in Lewes before reaching Eastbourne on the Friday. We'd then get the train home: simples!

Not quite. Chris wasn't as fit as he thought he was. Further, the weather on day two was atrocious, which, combined with the steep gradients, meant we couldn't even push our bikes uphill without sliding on the chalk, and, well, Chris pretty much died. Not literally, but he looked pretty dead.

I called it a day at lunch, north of Chichester, and we decided to find a pub to get warm, dry off and get some food before making our way home on the train, bus, taxi or whatever. One thing was for sure: he wasn't getting on that bike again.

135

We found a pub and walked in. It was posh. There we stood in the doorway, dripping wet, covered in mud, and all around were well-dressed people. Worse still, they were all sitting on pristine, white leather-backed chairs.

The landlord looked at us and, although he didn't say anything, I could tell he was caught between, *Hey, here's two more punters to help my cashflow,* and, *Are they really expecting to sit in my pub like that?*

I asked if there was a 'not so clean' table in the pub as we needed to eat. He had a wander around and proffered a little table for four in the corner, with, yes, you got it, white seats. Bless him. He could see we were tired, so I don't think he had the heart to turn us away.

We left our wet coats, helmets and gloves at the entrance and made our way over to the table. We didn't sit down; we took off to the toilets and started to get changed.

It was chaos. Chris just took all his wet clothes off and collapsed into a stall but left the door open so his bare legs were sticking out. He was exhausted. I was drying my body with paper towels; the sink was full of socks, shorts, gloves, dirt, you name it. There was mud everywhere. Had anyone walked in at that moment, I think they'd have just turned around and walked back out, proclaiming to the landlord, 'There's a couple of guys re-enacting a scene from a Village People backstage afterparty in there!'

As it happened, the landlord was very appreciative when we returned to our seats sporting clean jeans and dry shirts. Chris ordered a cup of tea and promptly put five sugars in it!

With the landlord's permission, we left the bikes locked to the pub. A bus, train and walk got us home for a shower. In the evening we went back to get the bikes in my car. Chris had slept and could hardly walk; his legs had seized up. The next day I went solo to complete the rest of the trip to Lewes.

They say every cloud has a silver lining, and this one did. Chris and I had a twin room booked in a hotel in Lewes. I called the hotel, which switched it to a double, and Lisa drove out to join me. We had a romantic meal, walk and night away in this picturesque old town.

Care for Veterans

Lisa went to Worthing's 'Artists Open Houses' event and came home excitedly saying, 'I think I've found the ideal place for you to volunteer at.'

After popping down to introduce myself, followed by an informal interview, I am now a weekly Thursday morning volunteer helping in the Care for Veterans social and recreation unit, where I do all sorts of activities such as making drinks, having fun and playing games with the residents, and usually all three.

I love it. To be completely honest, it takes me massively out of my comfort zone, but I think that's half the challenge. It also makes me count my blessings. I've just walked 500 miles. The residents here would struggle to walk five metres as most are in wheelchairs.

I am starting to form some relationships and feel like I'm making a connection with a few of the residents. It is so rewarding I am thinking about how I can carry on helping when I go back to work.

Impromptu downtime

I've been doing those jobs around the house I never get time for. I've even given myself some little projects. I've laid a new patio area for my barbecue; I've shaped and laid edging around my lawn. I also framed my complete Camino passport, along with a map of the route, and hung it in my lounge. The finishing touch was hanging the shell I had carried on my backpack on it, along with a little badge Evelyn bought me, a bookmark I was given, and, of course, *the* peg!

I'm currently painting the outside toilet floor, a job I've always procrastinated on. The weather has been brilliant, so I've even been out on my bike in between tasks to keep my fitness levels up, and the weight off.

Rather randomly, Lisa and I are off to Chris Evans's CarFest for the August bank holiday next weekend, our first ever festival. My golf handicap is coming down too, thanks to playing every couple of weeks with my friend Chris Sherman. Life feels good. I could get used to this.

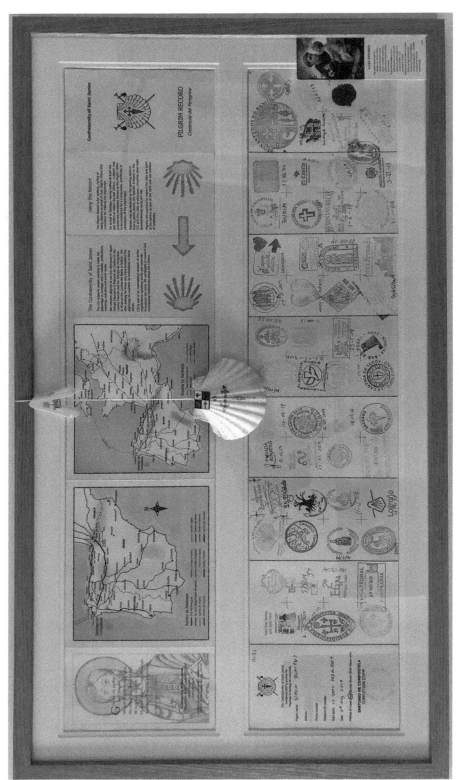

My framed passport, along with my shell and 'that' peg!

Thorpe Park with a twist

After the kids went back to school, Lucy had an inset day, which gave me an opportunity to spend the day with her doing something fun. She chose Thorpe Park.

The day turned out slightly differently to the one we planned.

Having been there a couple of hours I was taken ill, and it wasn't due to the rides. I was sick and felt absolutely awful, to the point I couldn't keep my eyes open over lunch. Lucy was the only one who ate, and she tucked into pizza that was making my stomach churn. I ended up in first aid and slept for about two hours.

At this point let me remind you Lucy has a visual impairment, she's twelve years old and she hates anything medical. When I asked her what she wanted to do, she naturally said what anyone else would have said in those circumstances: 'It's fine, Uncle. I can come to Thorpe Park again another day. I'd rather stay here with you, keep an eye on you and make sure you're OK.'

Of course she didn't! She was off. She made new friends and had the best time ever, apart from the fact that her parents, Cara and Chris, kept calling her to check she was OK.

I wasn't well enough to drive home, so Chris brought Lisa up to drive our car and me back, whilst Lucy went back with him. Thorpe Park is inside the M25, it was rush hour, and it took ages.

Looking back on our day out now, I think not only did it do Lucy the world of good (in fact I believe she had a better time as a result of my incapacity), but it was good for Cara and Chris too. They are not overprotective in any way at all, but it gave Lucy the chance to show them yet again what she is capable of, even with a visual impairment. That girl never ceases to amaze me.

Butlin's Bognor Regis

I'm not really a big fan of Butlin's, but this was a very special day. Look Sussex arranged for a whole bunch of their visually impaired kids and their families to get together at Butlin's Bognor Regis. It was a brilliant day and the kids loved it.

Look Sussex insisted that I come along to see how some of the money I had raised was being used. It made it all worth it. Those smiles. I had raised just short of £6,000, and thanks to Butlin's, who offered a deal for the charity, this was only a small dent in the overall budget. It's great to think that there will be many more events like this for these amazing kids. It was heartwarming, too, to have so many parents individually thank me for what I had done for the charity and their child.

Bruges

I have a circle of close friends locally, and whenever one of us has a significant birthday we mark the occasion. It started with all of our fortieth birthdays, and some second-marriage stag dos (which is inevitable, I guess, with this age group), and now, as some of us reach the fifties club, we're using it as an excuse to do the same. We've had weekends playing golf, days out in Brighton, weekends in Bournemouth, casino nights etc.

I was asked what I wanted to do, and I decided I'd like to go to the brewery that makes the Zot beer that I love so much. So that's what we did: eight of us one Saturday morning on the Eurostar to Bruges for lunch, brewery tour, more beers and then back to the hotel before dinner.

Evelyn, from the Camino, lives locally in Ghent, and she not only came to meet me but also booked a fabulous ribs 'n' beer restaurant that was a hit with the boys. She held her own with my mates too: quite impressive, really, considering we'd been drinking all afternoon. It was lovely to see her again.

A birthday present with a point to it

I was in my front garden when unexpectedly a courier arrived. Before handing me a parcel he demanded that I pay £160 import duty.

I noticed it had come from Mexico, so I called Camino Chris. 'I'm not sure what you've sent me, mate, but I don't know if it's worth more than £160.'

He just calmly replied, 'Man, it's worth much more than that.'

What on earth had he bought me?

After paying the courier I went indoors, curious and excited to open the package.

I laughed. I was also slightly shocked and a little bit scared. It was a knife. Of course it was! Not just any old knife, however. This was over a foot long; it had a handcrafted blade and a bone handle. It really was a beautiful piece of craftsmanship.

It was also a very fitting present, which Chris later told me he had purchased from Toledo, where he went after the Camino. Toledo is famous for steel, knives and swords, and to be honest this blade is so big it could probably qualify as a sword. It's the sort of thing you see in a movie, used to decapitate people. It's so sharp that I'm frightened to take it out of its beautiful leather sheath.

I received a message later that day. Chris had wired me the tax. He said, 'I can't have you paying for your own birthday present, now can I?'

Reaching fifty

I've had an amazing year, and what Lisa did for my fiftieth birthday was a fitting way to top it off. She totally surprised me with a Baltic cruise followed by three nights in Iceland, somewhere I've always wanted to go.

We had a fabulous couple of weeks together. We'd never cruised before and we loved it. One of our stops was in Copenhagen, and as soon as Søs realised we were heading to her home city she offered to be our local tour guide. It was great to meet her again and introduce her to Lisa.

I was in my element in Iceland, too. Having studied A-level geology, I was in awe of the place. I particularly enjoyed the geysers and walking between the North American and European plates. It was difficult to comprehend that they were still moving apart due to the volcanic activity below.

It would be my actual birthday the weekend after we got back, and I knew something was going on; either that or Lisa was having an affair, because the more we got into the cruise, the more she had to keep sneaking off to 'do things' on her phone.

As the weekend approached my mum and my brother's family came to stay. It was great. On the Saturday morning Mike, Jimbo, Rich and I went to play golf, so I finally got to take my brother around my local golf course. He might have let his brother win for his birthday, but no chance!

Brother-in-law Chris also caddied for me, which was hilarious. Chris is as good at golf as he is on a bike. Actually, come to think of it, he's worse at golf; much worse! He once played golf on one of our weekends away celebrating a friend's fortieth. He may have broken a world record that day, because we teed off at 11 am and we were still playing beyond 6 pm, wondering if we would ever get back in time for dinner.

It's a good thing he didn't keep us out so late this time, because when we returned home I was told to be ready to go back out by 2 pm. The only clue I had was that we were going on a train, but Lisa wouldn't tell me where. I presumed, as it was early afternoon, that we would be travelling to London. As we left the house, she said the trains were late, so we had time to pop into the Brooksteed for a quick drink.

I walked in to find sixty of my closest friends and family, who immediately burst into chorus with 'Happy Birthday' supported by Tom Carradine, a great act we know who does singalong classics on the piano. Wow. I hadn't suspected that. The whole pub was soon rocking and singing along to Tom's tinkling.

What an afternoon. The pub had even got Zot in on tap especially for me.

Afterwards, we decamped back to our house, where the party continued. Yes, all sixty of us! Needless to say it was messy, but a very, very special day spent with my amazing friends and family.

It was only about 1 am when someone mentioned a mojito. 'We have mojitos?' I enquired. Everyone laughed. Michael, James and their mates had been behind a makeshift cocktail bar in my kitchen all evening, creating and serving cocktails for everyone. I hadn't noticed. I'd been dancing, chatting, eating and drinking all day. No wonder everyone was smashed! Zot is strong, and with cocktails on top!

Martyn then made me sit down and let both of my boys make me a mojito, and I had to choose which was the best. I am not going to say who won. Not because I don't want to offend one of them; it's because I can't remember.

CHAPTER NINE

The End

It is now my final week before I return to work. I wouldn't say I'm ready to go back, but I do know that I can go back comforted by the fact that I've had the best six months of my life.

Some people say to me the time has flown by, but for me, thankfully, it hasn't. The weeks fly by when I'm at work due to the pace and complexity of everything I'm involved in, so in comparison this has been a serene time.

I will go back to work on Friday; yes, it just happens that 1 November falls on a Friday. I'll be refreshed and looking forward to the new challenges of a new team and a new role, but I have to be honest: I will really miss this lifestyle. I'm not looking forward to becoming a prisoner of time again, ruled by routine and a schedule where people can and will hijack my diary at the mere push of a calendar invite.

Work has been supportive of my volunteering and my boss has agreed that I can carry on with it on Thursday mornings as long as I make the time up elsewhere. That shouldn't be difficult to do; I normally put in well in excess of my required hours anyway.

Having a sabbatical is a fantastic way to prepare for retirement, and I recommend it to everyone. Further still, I now know I will really enjoy retirement, and I am sure of one thing: there is no way I am retiring after sixty. I intend to stop then or earlier if I can afford to. Life is too short. The Camino has served to remind me of the importance of life, love and cherishing the people who matter most, and I intend to take some of that spirit with me into my work.

On the other hand, I am very much looking forward to getting paid again in November!

Deep down the Camino has lit a candle somewhere within me, flickering constantly to remind me that there is more to my life than work. Maybe, just maybe, the near future will see a complete career change for me. Who knows?

31 October: Halloween

I feel a bit spooked, but not as much as I will tomorrow. It seems like years ago that Lisa and I were sitting on that beach in Sardinia where I was reading about the Camino, excited about my forthcoming break.

I've had some great messages today telling me to enjoy my last day of freedom; people really do care. I spent my last morning doing some admin and then went to Care for Veterans to play dominoes. I've been food shopping and also bought Lisa a thank-you card and flowers for when she returns home from work; after all, none of this would have been possible without her being 100% behind me.

Tonight, I'll cook dinner (again!). I'm doing one final slap-up meal as I've really enjoyed having the time to cook meals for the two of us and having dinner ready for when Lisa gets home from work. She's done it for me enough over the years, so it's been great to return the favour, plus I really enjoy cooking.

I wrote a sincere message in Lisa's card, and then, rather tongue-in-cheek, wrote this on the inside cover:

Going back to work will be tough because you'll now have to:

- empty the dishwasher every day
- do the shopping
- find a new PA!
- turn the beeper off on the washing machine (a pet hate of mine!)
- hang the washing out, and get it back in
- cook dinner, etc. etc. . . .

I've just dug out my laptop, work phone and building pass from one of the boys' wardrobes. It is getting real now: almost haunting, you could say. None of it will likely work tomorrow, and do you know what: if that's the case, I'm not going to worry about it.

Lisa and I still haven't shared our versions of our stories yet. I'm sure we'll have a good laugh over them. I get the sense mine has become mostly sincere with the odd bit of humour, whereas Lisa's might be taking the piss out of me with the odd bit of sincerity; we'll just have to see.

I wonder what she has written . . .

EPILOGUE

His Sabbatical

'I'm thinking of taking a sabbatical,' he said.

'Sorry?'

'I'm thinking of taking a sabbatical,' he said again.

I heard correctly the first time; I was just buying some time to process it. There had been mutterings in the past: 'Wouldn't it be good to have some time away from work? Not just holiday time but time to breathe, properly?' 'Three weeks is the longest holiday period I've had during almost thirty years' service.' 'You can apply for unpaid leave, you know.'

'OK,' I replied hesitantly. What I really wanted to say was:

When?

How long for?

Are you planning to disappear to the Himalayas to find yourself?

Are you coming back?

How much will it cost?

Is it really unpaid?

What will happen to your job in the meantime, and will there be a job to return to?

Will you really want to go back to work?

And, lastly, *What about me?* I'm not really a 'me' person, but my little brain started racing.

'Are you planning to travel?' I tentatively asked. This was a leading question, which would hopefully answer the majority of the others that were whizzing round my head.

'No, not really,' he said. 'I'd like to do El Camino from St Jean to Santiago, as you know – we'll come back to that – but I don't want to be away from you for too long and I won't have the money to waste on expensive travel. Plus, if I'm going to do any serious travelling, I'd want to share it with you, not go on my own.'

Well, that pretty much covered it. That was my Si.

Exciting discussions followed. Chewing the cud over an endless list of possible ideas for how Si would fill the days of his sabbatical after the Camino. He was going to walk the Camino first. He told me it should only take him five weeks to do the walk, so it left just short of five months for him to fill. Ideas continued to flow, and suddenly six months seemed such a short time to cram everything in.

The ultimate milestone was Si hitting fifty in October and, on the way, becoming fitter, both in body and in mind.

To be fair, Si only really had another four months to fill. He didn't know it yet, but October was going to be filled with surprises – hopefully welcome surprises – to celebrate the significant birthday.

Reactions from friends and family varied from, 'What a fabulous idea,' 'How lovely to take time out' and 'You deserve it' to the concerned, 'How will you manage for money?' 'What will happen to your job?' and 'Is it wise to take it?'

Then there was always the supplementary question addressed to me: 'So, what do you think about this, Lisa?'

Well, what did I think about it?

Well, I thought . . .

Selfish thoughts entered my mind: *Can I take six months too?*

Er . . . no.

I'm self-employed, and I run my own business. Without any employees, I am the business. Can't see any of my clients saying, 'Yeah, great, no problem, see you in November!'

So, once I had made that decision, it was full steam ahead to support Si. Plus I have had snatches of time off during my working life. OK, maternity leave isn't exactly a holiday, but it is time away from the hamster wheel of work. Two caesareans, one emergency and one elective, weren't exactly an easy route. But I have two boys, both of whom I'm immensely proud of, and it was definitely worth it.

I have always been a family person and deciding to have kids was a no-brainer. The only downside was my career. I had been successful, rising to the lower echelons of management in a finance role, and enjoyed working (funnily enough).

Being slightly old-fashioned in my approach to parenthood, I wanted to bring up my children my way, and I was in the fortunate position (with Si working) where as a family we could afford to do that. So I took a career break for five years and never went back full-time. A series of flexible roles around nursery and school term times, plus help from my mum, enabled me to keep my brain active and enjoy all the benefits of being a mum. So although life was busy, hectic at times, there was a good mix of work and pleasure: wife, mum, chair of PTA, school governor, part-time worker and, of course, I always found time to play netball.

Anyway, back to Si. He threw himself into being a great dad. We always had family holidays, action-packed weekends away, and the boys were always his focus. He spent ten years running James's youth football team, and he even became a qualified referee just so he could be on the pitch with our eldest. Sundays were always busy.

However, I didn't realise how many of the little things he had missed. I was always there for the school assemblies, sports days and parent consultations, and as the taxi driver for after-school activities, whilst improving my juggling skills and the art of producing and eating an edible meal within a twenty-minute window. Si's work has enabled me to play my life how I wanted, so now it seems only appropriate that I return the favour. Well, almost; the kids are independent young men now, but the sentiment is there.

All those early mornings knowing I wasn't the one jumping out of bed at the first alarm and I could safely catch another hour or two's sleep. Now it was his turn; well, at least for six months, anyway.

The Easter break was action-packed as usual. A full house, egg hunts, family trips out and some time together in the hot tub: a real treat. The start of the Camino (May) is getting closer and it's starting to become a reality.

El Camino de Santiago

The rucksack is almost packed; I wouldn't want to drag it to the boot of the car, let alone carry it on my back for five weeks.

Easter was a special pre-Camino time. Whilst on a day out with my family (and also with Si's mum), Si and Lucy went off to collect a special stone. It was to be placed at the base of the Cruz de Ferro, a special place along the route, and apparently a very emotional one. We also had to eat some seafood that I'd been instructed to buy, from a scallop shell. This is because, after we'd eaten it, Si was going to paint the shell and tie it to his rucksack. It's the sign of a pilgrim. We even rewatched *The Way* with Simon's mum.

Less glamorous parts of Si's preparation were the foot-rubbing ritual with the cream equivalent of surgical spirit, sleeping in a foot brace to help plantar fasciitis, and deciding which sunhat looked less ridiculous. The full-facial Sahara balaclava got outvoted (by me) in favour of the Australian outback one, minus the corks, of course.

Let me take you back to where it all started.

Lloyds Bank has a lot to answer for. It's where we met on an outward-bound pre-management course. Si has made some lifelong friends there and worked for some great leaders, one of whom was the inspiration for both the sabbatical and El Camino. Approaching retirement with ill health chomping at his heels was not the intended path for Neil. But life's a bugger sometimes, and you have to make the best and the most of it.

At the last count Neil has completed five pilgrimages to Santiago. A sincere family guy with a Catholic background, he set out on his first adventure to the tomb of St James. Si, being Si, wanted to support Neil, but with only a few holidays left he planned a short three-day trip, midway, just to check up on his friend. As it happened, he needn't have worried. Neil was apparently being well looked after by his new Camino family.

Si ventured onto the path with no preconceived ideas, and was definitely not looking for a religious experience. 'Agnostic' is the closest match for him, although he has always been supportive of the children being brought up in the Catholic education system. We even got married in a Catholic church.

I think it is fair to say that 'there was something going on' even on his three-day trip along the Camino. A few days after his return he wrote that poem. He was greatly moved by the whole experience. I keep thinking, *If all that happened in just three days, what effect will five weeks have on him?* Watch this space, I guess.

The outcome from his mini Camino was putting life in perspective; hence here we are at the start of a six-month sabbatical.

We've had a few conversations about being spiritual and not labelling yourself as religious. Si has always been spiritual; he's just not necessarily recognised it.

Interestingly, I chanced upon a quote from his Camino guidebook. It read,

'You are not a human being on a spiritual journey, but a spiritual being on a human journey.' How appropriate, I thought.

Tuesday 23 April: St George's Day

The countdown begins. There are eleven days left before El Camino starts, and only four days when Si will be working. It feels weird, like retirement at forty-nine without the big adjustment or payoff.

November seems a lifetime away, but the list of tasks I have in my mind for the stay-at-home husband is endless! In reality I suspect very little from my list will get tackled unless it appears on his as well. None of it is important; I am the world's best planner and, as everyone who knows me knows, I'm always thinking ahead. Not to say I don't enjoy the here and now; I just like to be super organised and make the most of life.

I'm currently sitting on the South Bank in London, sipping a glass of wine: the advantages of working for a client in London. My job is not usually this glamorous. I'm usually squashed onto the commuter train out of the city by now. Tonight is the first of many 'do's to celebrate his sabbatical with good friends.

The sabbatical begins

Friday 26 April was a surreal day for Si, who, with a big beaming smile, logged off from the working world; for a little while, anyway. Celebrations with friends, of course, ensued later on that evening at the Brooksteed Alehouse.

A busy final weekend with Si consisted of last-minute shopping, packing James off to university and a family lunch.

Monday morning was really weird. Si had until Thursday before he left. I was scrabbling around in the dark getting dressed with no alarm set for Si. Blocked from work emails, the wind-down had begun.

I came home from work and was pleasantly surprised. He'd had a productive day in the garden, designing and planting an alpine pot; he'd cooked dinner and was about to head off to his last Spanish lesson. I'm sure he has mastered enough vocabulary to get by.

The day of departure

This week has whizzed by. We sold our old American fridge (as you do), which meant a mad panic of emptying and scrubbing, followed by further scrubbing of the old one that's been in the garage for ten years, as the new one doesn't arrive for five days! Oh, yes, and there was a leak in the driveway that's now sorted. So much for a quiet few days before the big farewell.

We went to a local restaurant on our final night together. We joked that it was our Last Supper.

It's now 6 am and Si has just left amid a whirl of excitement as my crazy family ran down the road in their PJs to see him off. I'm now sitting, cup of tea in hand, gazing into the garden, watching the day wake up. The sun is breaking through, birds hopping in the purple shale and my favourite squirrel up to his *Mission Impossible* tricks. I take a breather in the silence. This is it. He's really gone. Tearful and proud, I tap away, typing my story.

Simon's Camino, week 1

Busy, busy, busy. A weekend decluttering at Si's mum's, catching up with friends, meals out and, yes, work!

Simon's Camino, week 2

We held a great fundraiser for Si at the Brooksteed Alehouse. I rewatched *The Way*. I then had a debacle as the new fridge was delivered but was too big to get through the kitchen door, and so it sat in the hallway.

I went to work, but also turned it into an opportunity for pleasure, catching up with more friends in London.

Simon's Camino, week 3

Consisted of gardening and work. Oh, and my neighbour and brother-in-law finally getting the fridge into the kitchen. Preparations were made for a trip to Barcelona with some friends. Life doesn't seem too bad being home alone!

Simon's Camino, week 4

Sangría and Gaudí in Barcelona, plus a little bit of unplanned rain. A quiet bank holiday for me, as all my family went to the Isle of Wight. I went for a fabulous cycle, appreciating the coastline, and enjoyed some me time.

A short working week – yippee.

Si's weeks are a stark contrast to mine. No work, for a start, although I wouldn't swap for the blisters, dodgy showers and sleeping in a dorm. I'm enjoying my own time too. Don't get me wrong, though; I'm racing around like a headless chicken ticking off items from my long task list.

It's great having Si's daily update on Polarsteps; I feel part of his journey and I'm loving it. Life can be very simple, but we sometimes like to overcomplicate it. I can tell that Si is relaxing his mind and letting life take its course. The support of friends has definitely boosted his effort.

The pilgrims' stories are endless, and it makes you realise how great and at the same time how hard life can be for some. There appears to be a lot of singing, laughter and wine; what more could he want?

Simon's Camino, week 5

Another countdown begins. The novelty of being in charge of my own destiny is wearing a bit thin now. Phone calls are great, but a cuddle would be so appreciated right now. I'm sitting on a packed train to the smoke, trying to get some enthusiasm for work as I continue to type my story.

Hopefully four more sleeps until I see Si, depending upon the weather conditions and state of blisters, of course. Santiago, here I come.

Santiago

My trip begins as his Camino ends. What a fabulous city Santiago is, full of love and happiness. The cathedral square is a special place. Pilgrims are continually arriving, some to outstretched arms, some just on their own, but all to a welcoming city.

I felt a bit of a fraud sharing the tail end of his experience, but it was a special time meeting other pilgrims who had a special place on Si's Camino, and we all celebrated in style.

The return

Back home with family and friends, the stories started to unravel and it was great to see the effect the Camino had had on Si. Five weeks was a short time, but so much had been gained.

The next four and a half months were great. Si mellowed into life at home, but El Camino was always close to his heart. Having never worn any jewellery except a watch and wedding ring, he is now sporting a silver Camino shell on a chain around his neck: a present to himself from Santiago. At least he didn't get a tattoo!

When Si came back from El Camino he told me he'd decided he wanted to do some volunteering. Whilst he was away I had toured Worthing with our good friend Steffie, for the Artists Open Houses event. One of the venues was a superb place called Care for Veterans and I told him all about it. He was chuffed with the recommendation and has since started working as a volunteer every Thursday, and he loves it.

An early birthday present for Si, and a late one for me, was a wonderful day at Ascot courtesy of Martyn and Lou. What a great event shared with lovely friends. Plus I came away with a decent win.

I have been planning Si's fiftieth present for what seems like forever. As I said, I like making plans, and for me this was the most stressful yet. It comes in three parts: a cruise, a party and a birthday lunch.

Although the cruise wasn't until October I decided to do a 'big reveal' earlier in the year, so that Si could share in some of the planning for trips and excursions. I had been prepared for a while, but then on a whim decided to reveal the surprise one evening in June. A hamper full of clues for the Baltic trip, which resulted in four hours of excited chatter and a couple of bottles of wine. I think it went down well. I'd intended to surprise him on the ship with the post-excursion to Iceland, but couldn't keep any more secrets. Well, perhaps just two more.

It was initially hard getting used to Si being around all the time. He kept popping up when least expected, but it was always lovely having dinner ready when I got in from work. Oh, how our roles had reversed.

The garden was looking good, as Si had been working hard, with a new edged border, beds decorated and planting accomplished. His golf handicap was slowly improving with more regular games, plus a trip to the Ashbury.

A holiday with Mum and Dad was a rarity and one we all thoroughly enjoyed. During our trip, we had a reunion with the ladies from Devon whom Si had met at the beginning of his walk. It was a fabulous evening hearing everyone's version of events, including the infamous 'goats of Pamplona' story. A video call with Chris in Mexico completed the early Camino gang reunion.

Si's fundraising has gone so well, breaking the £5,000 barrier: an outstanding achievement. A day spent at Butlin's with the children who will benefit from the funds raised brought it all into perspective.

With Si not working, we seemed to gain more time and the summer seemed to last forever. He spent the extra time with his family and friends. A trip to France with Jay for another Tour de France experience; Chilli Fest; Party in the Park and our first ever festival at CarFest. It wasn't a true festival experience, as we were driving in daily from a hotel, but, eh, you have to start somewhere, and if it hasn't got an en-suite I'm frankly not interested.

Si managed to squeeze in a weekend in Dorset for my birthday, visiting Monkey World. It was a fabulous time, but in the back of my head I was still organising his surprise party.

The cruise and trip to Iceland couldn't have gone any better. Experiencing the delights of the Baltic Sea and being spoilt by the service of Viking Cruises. Still managing to sneak a bit of time to deal with the last-minute preparations.

Leaving two days between arriving home, Si's family arriving and the actual surprise party was starting to feel a little bit too rushed. It didn't help when our youngest arrived home on the Friday night with a suitcase of washing. He was leaving again on the Sunday. Si didn't see a problem with hanging it around the house. I was having kittens, as I knew at least sixty people would be at the house the following day. Si was completely in the dark.

Party day arrived and we all managed to contain the surprise. I let out a huge sigh of relief when we arrived at the Alehouse and downed a large gin. No more surprises, except announcing that we were all going back to our house for an afterparty. Lots of laughter, and it was great to see all our friends and family in one place to celebrate the big event.

The next couple of weeks were busy with family birthdays and then the sudden realisation: this bubble was coming to an end. As the return to work loomed ahead, Si prepared himself. Was he ready? Would he transition smoothly? Would he have the same approach?

Let's wait and see.

There was something going on!

Acknowledgements

Huge thanks:

To **Neil O'Toole** for introducing me to the magic of the Camino.

To **Chris Lum** for unwittingly becoming my walking buddy and dear friend for life.

To **Stuart Blackburn** for humouring the idea in the pub, for seeing it through, and for always offering an alternative perspective to any situation.

To **Jayanti Limani** and **Bruce Hodgson** for being brilliant friends and for taking the time out to be a small but important part of my journey.

To my mum, **Jean Kettle,** for her undying love and support.

To **Look Sussex** for all that you do, and to **everybody who sponsored me** to allow them to do more.

And finally to **Lisa, Michael** and **James**, the best family ever.

CPSIA information can be obtained
at www.ICGtesting.com
Printed in the USA
LVHW071950021120
670493LV00027B/962